Seeking the End: Post-Apocalyptic Films 1916-2016

Nicholas D. Riccio

Seeking the End: Post-Apocalyptic Films 1916–2016

Copyright © 2018 Nicholas D. Riccio
All rights reserved.

ISBN: 978-0-692-09605-5

Book and cover design by Sarah E. Holroyd (http://sleepingcatbooks.com)

Image credits as follows:
Foreword and Chapter 2: *Martians vs. Thunder Child* is in the public domain (Henrique Alvim Corrêa [1876–1910]).
Chapter 5: Photo of George Street (taken from front of Polytechnic building on Stournari St.), Wednesday 10 Dec (after 4 days of riots). Photo was placed in the public domain by photographer Xenos2008.
Appendix A: Wall Street taken above steam stack road works, New York, February 2005. Photo was placed in the public domain by photographer Sparkx 11.
All other images, including those used on the cover, are used under Creative Commons CC0 License.

Dedication

All things are possible, but they are more possible when you have the support from the ones you love. My family has always been there for me, and encouraged me to try new things and even take risks. They were there when I considered new jobs, went into the rare book business, and even my decision to write this book had their full support. Anybody who thinks they can accomplish these things without the support and encouragement of their family is sadly mistaken. For that reason I dedicate this book to Mary, David, and Paul.

I also want to dedicate this book to John Zacherle, "the cool ghoul" who started me on this journey so many years ago.

Acknowledgements

There is no way I could ever have written this book without the encouragement of my wife, Mary. She gave constant support, and plenty of nagging, too. She even helped with some of the editing. While I have done more than my fair share of writing on financial subjects, Mary knows I have a real need for her grammatical help. She has always been a big help that way! My sons, David and Paul, also gave me support and feedback along the way, and seemed to enjoy my endeavor. I apologize to them for making them watch these movies as children. But guys, it could have been worse; it could have been soap operas. I would also like to thank my son Paul for helping out with the exploding world graphic, and Sarah Holroyd (Sleeping Cat Books), my editor and book designer, who did an impressive job pulling it all together.

It would be impossible to provide some of the film details I used without the Internet Movie Database (IMDb). I have a good memory, but not that good. When it came to finding release dates for films, and the names of characters and actors, that was my source. I also found a list of apocalyptic films on Wikipedia that was extremely helpful. While I did not use that list exclusively, it sure made the selection process for films a lot easier. It also brought to my attention a few films I'd never even heard of. I also found the chronological order of the Wikipedia list very helpful. Wikipedia was also useful when I had some difficulty in recalling some details about a film.

Foreword

doubt anyone could provide truly fair coverage for post-apocalyptic films. There are simply too many. However, I do think one can provide a good historical coverage and analysis of the subject by focusing on trends and a broad range of films. Certainly many of the major films in this genre will be covered, but so will some of the smaller films. Talking about *The Terminator* is obvious, but after watching it, so is the Australian film *These Final Hours.* Of course, when you are talking about a period of over 100 years, you are still going to find it challenging to pick the right films to focus on. A lot of stuff has been thrown our way between *Deluge* and *World War Z.*

Since it's always been hard for me to gain access and get comfortable with silent films, my focus will be almost exclusively on "talkies." I honestly don't know how big a deal that is, but readers should know the parameters of the subject I plan to cover. While I know there were some impressive sci-fi and horror flicks made during the silent era, such as *The Lost World*, *A Trip to the Moon*, *Nosferatu*, and *The Cabinet of Dr. Caligari*, I am only aware of one silent post-apocalyptic film: *The End of the World,* a Danish film made in 1916. The film can be seen on the

Internet, which is where I saw it. Now, I'm sure some may argue that *Metropolis* would fit the bill, but I saw that as more of a film about social evolution than a post-apocalyptic movie. Despite my disclaimer about silent films, I did include coverage of the Danish film, *The End of the World*, since it was the first of its kind. And I should also point out that I'm sticking with films made in English, thanks to poorly developed linguistic skills. And if it isn't already clear, I will stick with only films I have seen.

For the record, I have seen many of these films at least twice. Thanks to Netflix, Amazon Prime, YouTube, my local library, and my own DVD collection, I have taken another look at many of these films recently. So many films can lead to a little blurring, but I did my best to keep the facts straight. I even forced myself to finally watch *Waterworld*. One of the films I cover, *Alas, Babylon*, I believe I saw only once, many years ago. However, I have read the book twice, and did do an Internet search to refresh my memory on details. IMDb was very helpful in identifying the cast. Funny, even though I may not remember all the details, what I do remember is that it was this film, and the novel, that set the stage for my interest in post-apocalyptic movies.

As I went through the rich history of this film category, I'd like to believe I covered many of the major films in this genre. I also ended up including a number of films that I didn't know about until I started this journey. Again, thanks to Netflix and Amazon Prime, there were many others—maybe too many—that I had a chance to review as part of this effort. While many weren't all that interesting or particularly good to watch, there were some surprises in what I refer to as the "little post-apocalyptic flicks" that were quite enjoyable, and sometimes even thought-provoking.

I have presented the films by decade so the reader can get a sense of the evolutionary trends in this film category. However, within each decade, I have not always followed chronological order. I have some-times clustered the films by category, or because a major artist appears in more than one post-apocalyptic film. My placement may also repre-sent a focus on a new or important theme or film I wanted to highlight, as well as a less conspicuous place for less important films.

Since TV has also been a significant platform, especially over the past few years, for post-apocalyptic themes, I have included a chapter on

TV Apocalypse. This coverage spans 60 years from early *Twilight Zone* episodes, to made-for-TV movies, to *The Walking Dead*.

In an attempt to provide some useful feedback to potential film viewers, I have rated each of the films I covered in this book. The ratings go from one to five exploding worlds (as shown below), with five being the best. Almost a third of the films are average to below average; the other two thirds run from watchable to really worth seeing. Of course this is subjective, and one man's apocalypse may be another's stroll in the park.

Table of Contents

Introduction

In the early 1970s, I was spending the night in Queens, New York, when air-raid sirens went off, and I went into a panic. It seems a car had run into a pole that had a siren on it, and the siren went off. How do I find an air-raid shelter in Queens, of all places? Now, as a "baby boomer" who grew up during the Cold War, this may not be a particularly odd reaction. After all, didn't we come to the brink of nuclear war in the early 1960s during the Cuban Missile Crisis?

Sometime later, after some soul searching, I realized it was more than that. As a typically impressionable youngster, I had spent a good portion of my time watching sci-fi and horror films on TV and at the movies. I also read tons of sci-fi books. I didn't much care for Westerns or war movies; only monsters counted. I was a charter member of the Zacherley Fan Club. Zach was the host on the old *Shock Theater* and *Chiller Theatre* shows. I don't think as a child I ever paid to see any films that were not in this genre. But there was a price tied to this exposure. During the 1950s and '60s, within the sci-fi genre emerged the "end of the world" flicks that generally focused on nuclear war and its effects. No wonder I was always bracing for the attack. I think I can make a case that the Cold War fears of baby boomers played a major role in the ongoing popularity of post- apocalyptic movies.

While post-apocalyptic films didn't start in the 1950s, not to acknowledge their importance in establishing this genre would be silly. Even my mother knew that, always telling me I'd get screwed up watching those foolish movies. But the fact remains: many films with this angle poured out of Hollywood during this time. They were typically considered B movies, but often had a very talented cast, and sometimes a good script. Films like *Them!*, *The Day the Earth Stood Still*, *A Thing from Another World*, *The Blob*, *Invasion of the Body Snatchers*, *This Island Earth*, *Forbidden Planet*, *World Without End*, and *War of The Worlds* were top-notch sci-fi films, even if they were not all post-apocalyptic movies.

Still others, like *Five*, *When Worlds Collide*, *On the Beach*, and *The World, the Flesh and the Devil* were great films that clearly fit into the post-apocalyptic genre. Films that also belong to this genre, but are less notable, include the *Day the World Ended*, *Beginning of the End*, and *Robot Monster* (one I'd like to forget).

But it didn't stop with these films! Over the course of my life, I kept watching sci-fi films, and if I am a little screwed up now, maybe my fixation with these films is partially why. I loved films like *Panic in Year Zero*, *The Time Machine*, *Things to Come*, *Soylent Green*, *Night of the Living Dead*, *I Am Legend*, *World War Z*, and *Contagion*.

While it's easy to see the entertainment value of these films, they seem to reflect, at least to some degree, concerns with the real world. Starting with films like *Five* in 1951, our fears about the consequences of nuclear war have appeared in films for almost six decades. We came to understand and fear these consequences, as the struggle for survival was compounded by having to deal with a variety of mutated creatures from ants to humans.

In the 1960s, and continuing right through today, things other than nuclear war have emerged as possible threats to humanity. We now have to worry about viruses and diseases, new forms of radiation, electromagnetic pulses (EMPs), and climate change. This isn't so far-fetched. Our fears about the AIDS virus, Ebola, Zika, and swine flu were and are very real to a lot of people. The risks from EMPs, climate change, and catastrophic natural events have also not been lost on the human psyche. If you think I'm overreacting, try watching a few episodes of the *National Geographic's* popular TV show *Doomsday Preppers*.

From my perspective, the sociological value of post-apocalyptic films is far more than people would like to admit. On a very basic level, they do reflect our fears about the problems we believe exist in our environment. While I don't know how much of these fears, however subtle, affect our world view, it would be foolish to think they don't. During the Dark Ages, people believed we were headed for the end of days, thanks to the Black Plague and constant wars. It should not be surprising if you watch the six o'clock news that people might have a pessimistic view of the future, and our movies may reflect that pessimism. It becomes even scarier when you think about the increased output of these films in recent years. What does that say about us? While some may trivialize the vision embedded in sci-fi films, they are underestimating the power of these movies. As Jeff Rovin mentions in his book *Classic Science Fiction Films* (Citadel Press, 1993), to deny that these films have an important connection to reality "reflects a lack of constructive vision."

While there are all sorts of sociological and psychological implications of these films, that's not why I watch them. I just enjoy watching them, and, like the many sci-fi books I have read along the way, they often stimulate my imagination. When the character Harry Baldwin (Ray Milland) tried to save his family after a nuclear attack in *Panic in Year Zero*, I wondered what my family would do. How would anyone cope with flesh-eating zombies like the ones in *Night of the Living Dead*? Food for thought, but it boils down to a more basic thing; we simply like being scared to death watching these films. Filmmakers have been making them for over a hundred years, so there must be something to it.

Chapter One: Beginnings

The End of the World (Danish, 1916)

Over 100 years ago, a Danish film called *The End of the World* (translated title) became the first post-apocalyptic film (at least, as far as I've been able to determine). For a film that is about an hour and fifteen minutes long, it has a little bit of everything: a love triangle, class uprising, stock market manipulation, and, of course, the end of the world. It starts out in a mining town where two sisters, Dina and Edith West, get ready for a local dance. At the dance, Dina dumps her boyfriend and runs off with mine owner Frank Stoll. Edith is the good girl who ends up with a reputable sailor for a husband.

Our good friend Frank ends up being a big-wig in the stock market, and when news comes that a newly found rogue comet will bring destruction to the world, Frank buys stocks while everyone sells. (According to an article in Wikipedia, this film reflects the ongoing fears about Haley's comet, which appeared a few years before the film was made.) It seems that the astronomer who discovered the comet is related to Frank. When the astronomer and his colleagues conclude the Earth is doomed, they decide to hold this information back from the press to avoid panic. With all the cunning of Ivan Boesky (famous insider trading guy from the 1980s), Frank gets inside information from his astronomer relative about what's going to happen and releases some fake news that the comet does not pose a threat. Of course, the stock market goes up, and Frank makes a killing. I'm not sure why he cares about money at this point, since it's so difficult to spend during the apocalypse.

The comet arrives and basically trashes the Earth, causing flooding and earthquakes, and releasing poisonous gasses. Frank may have found a safe place in a mine, but Dina is killed in a gunfight during a class uprising when the comet starts to hit. Edith's husband, who is away at sea, is left alone. However, when he returns…all I can say is the film has a biblical ending when he returns to Edith, as one man and one woman face an uncertain future, but not without hope. So it would seem that the very first post-apocalyptic film is not about war or aliens, but trouble from the heavens. This theme would surface a number of times in the years to come.

The End of the World (French, 1931)

NR

While I have never seen the film, and don't want to spend a lot of time on it, I have to at least mention that it would appear the French film *End of the World* (*La Fin du Monde*), which was released in 1931 and directed by Abel Gance, was the first "talkie" to be considered a post-apocalyptic movie. According to IMDb (The Internet Movie Database) the plot is about what happens when people find out that the world is about to be hit by a comet in 114 days. It shows how different parts of society react to the news. It's interesting that the first two post-apocalyptic films had to do with comets.

Deluge (American, 1933)

The third film in this genre has a rather complicated history. The film is called *Deluge,* and it came out in 1933. For decades, the film was thought to be lost, but a copy dubbed in Italian was found in Rome in the 1990s. To be honest, I had never heard of the film, but found out about it a couple of years ago when I was looking for some unusual movies. While I'm not sure it's still available on the Internet, I managed to watch the entire film with English subtitles. It was directed by Felix E. Feist, and starred Peggy Shannon, Lois Wilson, and Sidney Blackmer. The cast was totally unfamiliar to me, which probably means they didn't have a lot of brand recognition.

Recently, according to reports on Amazon, the film is now available with the original English soundtrack. This is thanks to the efforts of Serge Bromberg with help from the Library of Congress, which located an original copy. I purchased a copy at a recent sci-fi convention and had the pleasure of seeing the film in English. Wow, what a difference! The film is impressive for a sci-fi flick made 84 years ago.

As far as the plot goes, the impact of earthquakes around the world leads to the destruction of the West Coast. Meanwhile, all these earthquakes and destruction elsewhere cause giant tidal waves to wipe out the East Coast, including New York City. Some folks have commented that the special effects of NYC getting trashed are not that impressive. I didn't think they were that bad for the period, and watching some of the buildings collapse unfortunately reminded me of 9/11. Some of the buildings appear to go straight down the way the Twin Towers did. I watched the Empire State Building fall, as did most of the buildings in New York City. However, it did look like the Statue of Liberty remained standing.

OK, earthquakes and tidal waves nearly destroy the world, but some people survive. Some are good; some not so much. This theme has been present in nearly every post-apocalyptic film over the past eight decades. This probably reflects a basic truth about human nature. Aside from the destruction, which took mankind back to the dark ages, there was a sub-plot in the film.

Our hero is Martin Webster (Sidney Blackman), who survives the devastation after trying to save his family, but he is separated from them and thinks they are dead. He ends up in a shack near a cave trying to collect provisions. Meanwhile, a female swimmer, Claire Arlington (played by the very lovely Peggy Shannon), is rescued by two brutes after she swims to their little island. Claire seems to spend half the movie running around in her underwear. Well, these two brutes have only bad things on their minds about Claire. One brute kills the other, and Claire swims to another place, where she is rescued by Martin.

They hang out together, and eventually fall in love, and, after being saved from an attack by thugs, are brought to the town where good people reside. The plot thickens as Martin finds out his wife and kids are still alive. Now Martin has two women he loves, and struggles with what to do. He eventually becomes leader of the town, but Claire finds the situation too difficult to bear. In the final scene of the movie, she swims away by herself, while Martin watches from the bank. All in all, it is a powerful movie, and the first of its kind made in the United States. The film may seem a little dated, but it does capture the essence of these films: devastation, followed by the struggle for survival, and the range of human reactions to the unthinkable.

Things to Come (British, 1936)

Three years later, in 1936, *Things to Come*, one of my all-time favorite films from this period, was released. The film was based on the H.G. Wells novel *The Shape of Things to Come*. I first saw the film when I was around 12 years old on TV. I remember being fascinated by the eerie black and white images, sets, special effects, and excellent performances by the actors. After *All Quiet on the Western Front*, I consider this film a very powerful post-WWI anti-war movie.

In any case, the film had an outstanding cast, including Raymond Massey, Ralph Richardson, Cedric Hardwicke, and Ann Todd. And how can you go wrong with a movie based on the work of H.G. Wells? The storyline is about a decades-long war that starts in 1940. The fighting continues, year after year, even though no one remembers how the war started, and society eventually breaks down. As a youngster watching this film for the first time, I was most intrigued when a plague destroys most of the people who are left. I believe the plague was called the "wandering sickness," and people were shot on sight when they showed symptoms. As I recall, people would get up and start walking with their hands stretched out in front of them, and had crazed looks on their faces. My friends and I talked about what it might be like to live in a society like that. I'll bet there are more than a few kids today talking about how they would cope with a zombie epidemic.

By 1970, a strongman dictator emerges, appropriately called the Boss (Ralph Richardson), who is a primitive chap with little interest in improving his society. John Cabal (Raymond Massey) shows up representing a new civilization called Wings Over the World, which was originally started by scientists and engineers. To make a long story short, they take out the Boss and his people with some kind of sleeping gas. A new era of progress begins, and mankind heads for a "golden age" without war. Despite considerable technological and social progress, their civilization becomes divided on the subject of progress. A group headed by Theotocopulos (Cedric Hardwicke) wants people to have a rest from progress, while Oswald Cabal, the son of John Cabal, heads a group that wants to move forward.

At the end of the film, Cabal's daughter and her boyfriend take a trip to the moon, while half the population tries to trash their spaceship. The final scene where Raymond Massey delivers a speech to a colleague, points to the stars, and reminds his friend about the need for man to move forward is one of the most impressive scenes I have ever seen in a sci-fi movie. Despite the chaos going on around them in this film, as the ship takes off, the film leaves the viewer with a hopeful message about the future. Most of the films in this genre that followed this movie do not have that optimism.

For the remainder of the 1930s and 1940s, that was it with respect to post-apocalyptic movies. Sure, Universal Studios and others still cranked out many horror and sci-fi films like *The Invisible Man Returns*, *The Ape Man*, *The Mad Ghoul*, *Dr. Jekyll and Mr. Hyde*, and *The Wolf Man*, but they didn't release much in the post-apocalyptic department. Not surprisingly, WWII did not leave much room for that kind of movie; they were dealing with the real thing.

Chapter Two: The 1950s

Five (American, 1951)

If we fast-forward 15 years, the lack of post-apocalyptic films ended with the onset of the 1950s. The film that lead the way was Arch Oboler's *Five*, which was the first film about the impact of nuclear war. I have only seen the film twice, but I found it rather impressive in a creepy kind of way. First, it was the first movie about nuclear war, and, second, it was probably one of the few films of this period that presented an African-American actor on an equal footing with his white counterparts. Joachim Boaz, in an excellent article on the film ("A Film Rumination: Five," Arch Oboler [1951]), correctly points out that this film is dark for the period. Bleak and depressing also work for me. But I was fascinated by the story, and despite the low budget and somewhat unknown cast (at least to me), it seemed real. I found the trailer for the film a little on the sleazy side—you know, four men, one woman—but you do have to sell tickets.

The plot focuses on five people who survive an A-bomb and the fallout that wipes out the rest of the human race. The survivors are Michael (William Phipps), Roseanna (Susan Douglas Rubes), Eric (James Anderson), Charles (Charles Lampkin), and Mr. Barnstaple (Earl Lee). While they start from different places, they end up at a hillside house. Michael takes to Roseanna. Hey, what's not to like? She *is* the last woman on Earth. But Roseanna, pregnant and in shock, isn't initially in the mood for him. Mr. Barnstaple, an elderly banker, and Charles show up to join the party, and they eventually pluck Eric (who was climbing mountains when the bomb hit) out of the sea to become "five."

In addition to his mountain-climbing skills, Eric is also a racist, and gets into it with Charles, the lone African-American survivor. In the end, Eric kills Charles, and trashes their farming efforts. Along the way, the elderly banker dies, and Roseanna agrees to go with Eric into the city to find her husband. Good old Eric gets radiation sickness, and runs off into the sunset. Roseanna finds her way back to the house—after losing her baby—and reunites with Michael. So now they live the Adam and Eve scenario, but with a touch of radiation.

A number of films with variations of this plot would appear over the next two decades, but I still find this an amazing film. It was made only about six years after the first bombs were dropped on Japan, and despite its low budget, it gives a sad but realistic view of the consequences of nuclear war. No matter what criticisms you can hurl at this movie, it was a film of incredible vision.

When Worlds Collide (American, 1951)

The next noteworthy film in this genre, *When Worlds Collide*, was also released in 1951. This is one of my favorites from the 1950s batch, and I love watching it. It has a great cast, great script, and the film actually won an Oscar for special effects. While you may not know their names all that well, cast members Richard Derr, Barbara Rush, John Hoyt, Frank Cady, and Larry Keating were fixtures in films and TV shows from this era. I always liked John Hoyt, who, like Whit Bissell, seemed to be in so many films from this period. He was in *Spartacus*, *The Blackboard Jungle*, and even had time to do a *Twilight Zone* episode or two.

Unlike *Five*, it isn't nuclear war that threatens mankind in this film; instead it's a planet or star (Bellus) that is on a collision course with Earth. The findings reported by scientists concerning this calamity are confirmed by Dr. Cole Hendron (Larry Keating). He hires pilot David Randle (Richard Derr) to fly to the U.S. to share his findings with other scientists. There is skepticism about Hendron's findings, but a couple of nice rich guys give Hendron money to build a spaceship. Somewhere nearby is planet Zyra, which Hendron hopes will be a place to give what's left of the human race a second chance.

That's the good news; the bad news is that Hendron doesn't have enough money to pull it off. Enter not-so-nice rich guy Sidney Stanton (John Hoyt), who will give Hendron the funds he needs if Sidney gets a place on the spaceship. During all this drama, pilot David Randall finds time to get romantically involved with Hendron's daughter, Joyce (Barbara Rush). Now, when the crap really starts hitting the fan, the folks selected to be on the ship (mostly drawn by lottery) are boarded into it. Hendron pulls a fast one and keeps Stanton from getting on the spaceship in order to give everyone a better chance to make it to Zyra. It's a close call, but they make it to Zyra, and with a little help from George Pal's special effects, mankind gets its second chance. Compared to *Five*, this is a far more hopeful ending.

War of the Worlds (American, 1953)

In 1953, *War of the Worlds* was released, and for my money this was one of the best sci-fi flicks from the 1950s. In fact it almost made my top ten list. *War of the Worlds* is another flick inspired by an H.G. Wells novel, so as I have said before, how can you go wrong? Many 1950s sci-fi films are dismissed as lesser quality events and B-list films, often with second- or third-tier actors. Sure, some are rather cheesy, and many may have low budgets, but the scripts and actors are often top notch. In the case of *War of the Worlds*, none of the usual criticisms apply. The movie had a decent budget, and you only have to check out the special effects to see that. Also, the film has a great cast headed by Gene Barry as Dr. Clayton Forrester. What starts out as an entertaining sky show of shooting stars ends up as a full-scale global alien invasion.

Now, not to let the cat out of the bag, but when those pesky aliens fry Pastor Matthew Collins (Lewis Martin), you know their fate is sealed. However, before that happens, the aliens (who are considered Martians) start taking over and basically destroy the Earth. Of course, we try to fight back, and Dr. Forrester and his girlfriend, Sylvia (Ann Robinson), actually manage to whack an alien in a farmhouse, and take its technology to be evaluated by other scientists.

We use guns, tanks, planes, bombs, and even the atomic bomb, but nothing works. So the aliens continue trashing everything in their path. As they continue their rampage, destroying cities around the world, they make big mistake number two. They mess up a church while they are wreaking havoc. Their ships start crashing and they all die. The storyline tells us that their lack of immunity to Earth's diseases is what did them in, but I'm not sure that God wasn't more than a little ticked off after they destroyed a church and fried a minister. Some people have suggested the film reflected the realities of the cold war. I'm not all that sophisticated; I just saw a good monster movie that I loved.

Robot Monster (American, 1953)

Another 1953 release was *Robot Monster*. While this is a post-apocalyptic film, I thought it was stupid when I was nine or ten, and it hasn't gotten better with age. If you watch it, watch with a group and do some serious drinking. Robot (Ro-Man) is really a guy in a gorilla suit who wipes out the human race except for one family. But since he develops a romantic interest in the daughter of the last family, which he needs to take out, he is conflicted. The movie has death rays, and even prehistoric monsters show up, but in the end it's just a dream had by Johnny (Gregory Moffett), the little boy in the story, who banged his head. The kid wakes up and his family is fine. But Ro-Man steps out of a cave at the end to keep you guessing. I'm still trying to figure out why the film included stock footage of the dinosaurs from the film *One Million BC*.

Them! *and* Invasion of the Body Snatchers (American, 1954, 1956)

Them!

Invasion of the Body Snatchers

There is always a gray area in life, and this applies to post- apocalyptic films too. *Them!* and *Invasion of the Body Snatchers* are in that gray area. In *Them!*, giant mutant ants threaten mankind, but Dr. Harold Medford (Edmund Gwenn, who played Kris Kringle in *Miracle on 34th Street*) and FBI agent Robert Graham (James Arness, who played Marshall Matt Dillon on *Gunsmoke*) take out the ants before they do too much damage, so we never actually get to that post-apocalyptic state. Along those same lines is *Invasion of the Body Snatchers,* released in 1956, a far more complex film that some people feel reflects the paranoia of the day. Once again, it was just a good sci-fi flick to me. That's the nice thing about seeing these films for the first time when you are a kid.

As far as *Invasion of the Body Snatchers* is concerned, to make a long story short, giant pods from outer space (at least I think they are from space) produce replicants of people. These replicants take all the memories and physical appearance of the person once they fall asleep. But they become robot-like and devoid of emotion. Dr. Miles Bennell, excellently played by actor Kevin McCarthy, attempts to get to the bottom of complaints from patients that their loved ones are not who they appear to be. Miles and girlfriend Becky Driscoll (Dana Wynter) try to figure out what's happening. Once they realize the situation, they try to warn people. Becky doesn't make it after falling asleep and becoming one of them, so it's left to Miles to go it alone. While he manages to get out of town, nobody in the next town believes him, and he seems to be headed off to a mental hospital. However, a truck loaded with these giant pods has an accident on the highway, and we are saved from the pods. Whit Bissell, who seems to have a bit part in every movie made from 1950 to 1960, has a small role as a psychiatrist.

The Day the Earth Stood Still (American, 1951)

Another flick that falls into that gray area is *The Day the Earth Stood Still*, released in 1951. Since the aliens were good aliens, and not many people got eliminated, I excluded this as a full-fledged post-apocalyptic film. I'm sure some would argue the point that any time aliens threaten to wipe out our planet, it should be a go. But these guys really just warned us; they already knew we were intellectually challenged, and they didn't really want to take us out. But it was a great film with a great cast that included Michael Rennie, Patricia Neal, Hugh Marlowe (a major sci-fi star in the 1950s and 60s), Sam Jaffe, and Bill Gray from *Father Knows Best*.

World without End (American, 1956)

Released in 1956 was another one of my favorites, *World Without End*. OK, the special effects are a little shaky, and that rocket ship sequence when they break the time barrier is a little much, but it has a great cast and a good script. Hugh Marlowe, who plays John Borden, was a really accomplished actor who had a great start, but seemed to be relegated to B sci-fi flicks. He had an important role in the film *Twelve O'clock High*, but was doing *Earth vs. The Flying Saucers* a few years later. The cast also included Rod Taylor, who would go on to have an amazing career in film. This was the first film I saw him in.

I saw this film so many times I used to recite the gibberish mutant language to my friends. Sadly, I was still doing that in college. The plot is simple. Four guys go into space to orbit Mars, and break the time barrier on the way back. They crash-land on an unknown planet, and begin to survey their new home. They stumble on a cemetery, and realize they are back on Earth a few hundred years into the future. An atomic war seems to have wiped out the human race.

Not a good situation, but things are about to get worse. As they attempt to explore their world, rather unattractive mutant creatures attack them. They are kind of like one-eyed cavemen. In their attempt to escape, the four men find a cave that leads to an underground city where normal humans live—well, semi-normal, anyway. This is an advanced society of people who have lived underground for centuries, and are afraid to come out.

Our hardy twentieth-century heroes won't have this, and after some drama, which includes winning over some of the very attractive futuristic women in short skirts, they begin an expedition to the surface. After kicking some ugly mutant butt, they send the bad guys away, keep the not-so-ugly ones with them, and start a new world on the surface. While I'm poking a little fun at the plot, it was a wonderfully acted and executed film.

Day the World Ended (American, 1955)

A far less impressive film of this genre was Roger Corman's *Day the World Ended*, released in 1955. Once again, we are down to seven people after an atomic war. Of course, we have the threat of radioactive contamination and a mutant creature that seems to want to kill everything. And, of course, we have a battle between Richard Denning and Mike Connors for the affections of Louise, who is the rancher's daughter. The cast isn't bad—I have always respected the work of Denning, especially his performance in *The Creature from the Black Lagoon*—but the plot is thin, special effects limited (which is a very kind way to put it), and I found the film very hard to get into. I have seen the film only twice, and didn't make it through the second time. IMDb indicates it took nine days to make the film; perhaps that was eight days too long.

The World, the Flesh, and the Devil (American, 1959)

A classier movie was the 1959 film *The World, the Flesh, and the Devil*. However, this was hardly a candidate for the post-apocalyptic hall of fame, as it was often tedious and slow moving. The movie had a small cast (three people), but how can you lose when that means Harry Belafonte, Inger Stevens, and Mel Ferrer? Harry Belafonte gives a fine performance, and manages to side step most of the racial stereotypes of the day. He is a man of great pride and skill, but also sensitive to social conventions. When Sarah Crandall (Inger Stevens) blurts out she is free, white, and over 21 in a discussion with Ralph Burton (Belafonte), he gets the message, even if that's not the one Sarah wants him to hear.

After being stuck in a cave for a few days, Ralph Burton emerges to find mankind wiped out by an atomic war. Sound familiar? He heads to New York City, where he hooks up with Sarah Crandall. They become good friends, but you know an attractive man and woman can't be left alone in these films, so in pops Benson Thacker (Mel Ferrer). Thacker sets his sights on the lovely Sarah (no surprise there), and despite Burton's efforts to keep his distance, conflict results. So now you have three people left on Earth, and two of them end up trying to kill each other.

In the end, peace prevails and the three march off into an unknown sunset. The film was mildly entertaining, and well acted, but I found it hard to really get into it. Perhaps the plot was a little old, and rather shallow. While I saw the film again when I was older, my opinion didn't change much.

The Lost Missile (American, 1958)

Another one of those less-than-stellar flicks that almost got by me was the somewhat obscure *The Lost Missile,* released in 1958. Until recently, I didn't know this film existed, but as I was checking through various lists on the Internet, this one popped up. It includes Robert Loggia in his first starring role as Dr. David Loring. The film is probably another one not destined for the post-apocalyptic hall of fame. The menace to mankind is an unknown rocket or missile that seems to destroy everything in its path by generating intense heat. They send planes to shoot it down, but those only manage to get fried, too.

Panic is setting in, and Ottawa and New York are next on the missile's path. There is plenty of stock footage used in this flick, and while scientists try to figure a way to stop it, New York City decides to get all the children out of the city in school buses. While Dr. Loring (Loggia) tries to find a solution, his friend's wife has a baby in a fall-out shelter, his girlfriend dumps him (at least for a short time, because he is obsessed with work), and people are panicking all around them. In one scene, you see people going nuts on a subway platform, and one woman gets electrocuted on the third rail. Meanwhile back at the ranch, Ottawa gets fried, as Dr. Loring develops a nuclear rocket material that can take out the unknown missile. Actually, people seem to know the missile is from outer space. As he heads to the launch site for our save-the-world missile, some young punks steal his jeep with the nuclear material.

The dopey punks open the box with the nuclear material and die, and Dr. Loring exposes himself to the stuff to get it to the launch site. He makes it in the nick of time, saves the world, and dies of radiation poisoning. This film is hardly a classic, and I think Robert Loggia's talents were kind of wasted in this one, but, if nothing else, humanity prevailed over some really sneaky aliens.

On the Beach (American, 1959)

We end the decade with the very powerful film *On the Beach*. It was a long time ago, so I don't remember if I read Nevil Shute's book or saw the movie first. But I was taken with both! Directed by Stanley Kramer, the film has a wonderful cast that includes Gregory Peck, Ava Gardner, Fred Astaire, and Anthony Perkins.

The film is set in the early 1960s, when a nuclear war takes out North America, and then some. But an American submarine is near Australia, so it escapes the carnage. While Australia has avoided the initial impact from the blast, the radiation is coming for them. Unlike most doomsday atomic war films, this one highlights the reality of facing the horrors of radiation they can't stop, but have months to think about.

People try to live some form of a normal life, but they all know they are facing inevitable death. Peck's and Gardner's characters start a romance; Astaire's character gets into racecars and pushes it to the limit. Watching Anthony Perkins's character and his young wife and child face the grim reality is probably the most difficult part of this movie. Perkins has to go so far as to explain to his wife how to kill their child. While Peck may want to stay with Gardner, his crew wants to head home, so he leaves her to lead his men back to the U.S.

Astaire's character commits suicide by carbon monoxide poisoning, and the Australian government provides suicide pills for everybody else. The final scenes show Melbourne as a ghost town, indicating that everyone there is dead. What is most frightening about this movie is that you can feel the depression setting in as people face their doom. There is no hope here, not even for children. A very powerful story!

So ends the 1950s. Post-apocalyptic films were an important part of the incredible sci-fi output of that decade. While the special effects of later years would dwarf those of the 1950s, the storytelling of many of these films can stand with the best of recent films. Films like *This Island Earth*, *It: The Terror from Beyond Space*, *Them!*, *Forbidden Planet*, *The Thing*, *The Blob*, *The Creature from the Black Lagoon*, and *Invasion of the Body Snatchers* have held up well, and I think hold their own with later sci-fi movies.

Chapter Three: The 1960s

The Time Machine (American, 1960)

We can start the 1960s off with one of the most-loved sci-fi films ever made, *The Time Machine.* Released in 1960, this film has an outstanding cast, great direction, and a truly wonderful script, based on the H.G. Wells novel of the same name. While I own a couple of copies of this film, I still find it hard not to watch when it's on TV. Between the book and the film, this movie and two others (*Panic in Year Zero* and an old TV show *Alas, Babylon*), shaped my lifelong interest in post-apocalyptic films.

Before I talk a little about the plot, I have to make some acknowledgement of the wonderful cast, which included Rod Taylor (remember him from *World Without End*), Alan Young (AKA Wilbur from the TV show *Mister Ed*), Yvette Mimieux, Sebastian Cabot, and the ever-present Whit Bissell. While I don't know if he would have agreed with me, I have always thought this was Rod Taylor's best film. As far as special effects go, they were fairly impressive the first time I saw the film, and I think they hold up well. Remember, comparing 1960's technology to today isn't really fair. Sure, the Morlocks were scarier in the 2002 remake of the film, but the stop-action sequence when Rod Taylor kills one in the cave as he tries to escape was cool. You can see it disintegrate as he goes forward in time.

After demonstrating a miniature time machine to his friends at a dinner party in 1900, George (Rod Taylor) announces he has a bigger machine almost ready to go. They are more than a little skeptical, and his friend David Filby (Alan Young) warns him not to mess with this stuff. George ignores his friend, sets up a dinner party for a week later, and heads off into the future. George is unhappy with his time, and hopes the future will offer a better chance for mankind.

So George begins his journey, and makes his first stop in 1917, where he meets his friend David's son, James. He learns that David has died in the Great War, so he resumes his journey. He pauses in 1940 to find England facing bombing during WWII. He decides to move ahead again and stops in 1966 to admire human progress. While visiting 1966, he runs into an elderly James Filby, who doesn't recognize him at first. James is shocked that George has not aged in all those years. Their visit is interrupted by an atomic war, which basically destroys civilization. Funny, I can remember talking with my friends about the film, and we wondered if 1966 would be the end for us all.

In any case, George escapes the catastrophe by putting years between him and the atomic war. Some 800,000 years into the future he stops again, finding what seems to be a serene landscape. However, he discovers that humanity has evolved into two groups: the Eloi, childlike snooks who don't have a clue, and cannibalistic Morlocks who eat the Eloi.

George is disgusted with the dopey Eloi, who have let civilization go down the tubes, although he does take a liking to the lovely Weena (Yvette Mimieux), whom he saved from drowning a little earlier. Meanwhile, the Morlocks have taken his time machine. While George tries to figure out how to get it back, the Morlocks do a cattle call and some of the Eloi march toward their doom. But George helps them fight back, and the Eloi escape.

After fighting a few more Morlocks, George retrieves his time machine and heads back to his own time. At a dinner party with his friends, he tells his story, but finds them rather skeptical. George goes back to the Eloi, and when David Filby asks the housekeeper if George took anything with him, we find he has taken three books. We are meant to ponder—and I'm still wondering—which books he took on his return. I could never do justice to this wonderful film in such a short summary, but it is truly storytelling at its best.

Last Woman on Earth (American, 1960)

From the sublime to the ridiculous, we have the *Last Woman on Earth*, also released in 1960. Kind of a knock off of *The World, the Flesh and the Devil*, this film features two men and a woman. While scuba diving in Puerto Rico, a man and his wife surface to find everybody dead. It appears that something destroyed the oxygen, at least temporarily. When another man joins them, a love triangle begins, and to make a long story short, the husband eventually kills his competition, and the two are left to await their fate. This is one of the few films in this genre I have seen only once, or maybe twice: message there!

The Last Man on Earth (Italian, 1964)

Not to be sexist, but *The Last Man on Earth*, staring Vincent Price, was a much better movie. Released in 1964, made in Italy, and set in the year 1968, this was kind of a zombie-vampire flick. Price's character (Dr. Robert Morgan) is the only person to survive a plague that turns people into a kind of vampire. They can't go out in the sunlight. Morgan becomes a vampire slayer and hunts them during the day. Price's character is almost robotic, as depression and a bleak occupation make him seem almost lifeless himself.

On one of his treks, he spots a woman named Ruth, and while they are suspicious of each other, she returns with Morgan to his home. He learns that some of her people have a vaccine that allows them to function more or less normally with the drug—not so much without it. Dr. Morgan, being basically a good guy, cures Ruth with a transfusion of his blood. While things are looking up on the domestic front, some of Ruth's zombie-vampire friends find Morgan and eventually kill him after a gunfight by impaling him in a church, despite Ruth's efforts to save him. According to indiewire.com and other sources, *The Last Man on Earth* (along with a few other movies) was based on Richard Matheson's book *I Am Legend*. The gritty black and white texture of this film, along with a strong performance by Vincent Price, made for a great flick.

Panic in Year Zero (American, 1962)

For reasons I can't totally explain, the film *Panic in Year Zero* (1962) is one of my all-time favorites in the post-apocalyptic genre. Sure, it has a strong cast and a good script, but it certainly isn't a big budget film, and from a technical or special effects standpoint it isn't that special. But for some reason, it felt very real to me, and I often wondered how my family would have fared in this scenario. Also, this film brings us back to an atomic war story line, which was a very real possibility when the movie was released.

The cast includes Ray Milland (who also directed it), Jean Hagen, Frankie Avalon, and Mary Mitchel. The film starts out with the Baldwin family getting ready to leave suburban Los Angles on a camping vacation. While the family is driving along, they see bright lights coming from behind them. You get the feeling they know what happened, but are reluctant to admit it at first. Ann Baldwin (Jean Hagan) convinces husband Harry (Ray Milland) to return home to find family members.

That becomes a very short-lived goal as Harry decides, against the objections of his wife, that for his family to survive, they must head for the hills. Harry believes—correctly—that civilization will fall apart. This happens all too soon, and he has to protect his family. He starts this process by finding an out-of-the-way town to get supplies. Harry ends up brawling with a hardware store owner when Harry doesn't have enough cash to pay for his purchases. His wife thinks he is behaving like a hoodlum, but Harry feels he has to if they are going to survive. They even manage to move into a cave to stay protected.

Harry's fears turn out to be well founded. His daughter is raped, and his son is shot by one of the punks who tried to terrorize his family earlier. Before his son is shot, Harry and son dispense some "frontier justice" on the thugs who raped his daughter. However, they also manage to save a young woman who had been held captive by the thugs. After his son is shot, Harry seeks out a local doctor, who insists the boy needs a transfusion if he is to survive. Harry heads to a military base to get help, and is confronted by the military along the way. They direct him to a specific location, and, as the family leaves, the soldiers acknowledge to each other that there go five good ones, meaning they were not exposed to radiation.

You have to admire Harry's resolve when faced with the unthinkable. He manages to save his family from a nuclear war, and has the presence of mind and skills to really protect them after the bombs are dropped. I think this movie also started the "prepper movement," so if you are one of those people who stocks up on supplies to deal with disasters, you have Harry Baldwin to thank for it.

This is Not a Test (American, 1962)

Thanks to Amazon Prime, I recently discovered a film called *This is Not a Test,* released in 1962. Like *Panic in Year Zero,* and released in the same year, this film is about nuclear war. However, the similarity ends there, as *This is Not a Test* would hardly be put on anybody's must-see apocalypse film list. The cast is largely unknown to me, and the script is another one of those Cold War scare flicks. We start out with a lonely highway patrolman who is ordered to stop all traffic from moving toward the city. It is early in the morning, so traffic is light, but the characters he meets make up for the small numbers. We have a truck driver, a drunk or two, a murderer, an adulteress, a degenerate gambler, and a grandpa and his granddaughter.

The policeman who is trying to save this motley crew is a jerk, a bully, and a rather sadistic chap who seems to like pushing people around. Anybody who can kill a small dog because it is breathing too much is no Mother Teresa. He gets the idea he can save people by putting them into an emptied trailer. He plans to keep them there for two weeks, and while they have some food and water, crap hits the fan in short order.

One guy kills himself, primarily because his wife has taken up with the truck driver. The drunk starts to disrobe after just a few minutes in the trailer, and at that point the cop kills the dog to save on air. A few looters show up, steal a car, some supplies, and a woman, but in the end they all appear to get fried by a nuclear blast. However, gramps and his granddaughter, along with a young man, go off on their own. Gramps tells the youngsters they can survive in an old mine he used to play in when he was a kid. That represents the hope for tomorrow. This was a low budget flick with a nearly no-name cast who were not that bad, but the movie wasn't much to write home about; the story didn't do much for me.

The Day of the Triffids (British, 1963)

While nuclear war was a big deal in 1960s post-apocalyptic flicks, new sources for problems facing humanity also surfaced. In 1963, the British film *The Day of the Triffids* was released, which was about most of humanity being blinded by a weird meteor shower, and giant man-eating plants (Triffids) attempting to dominate the world. It sounds a little silly, but I really enjoyed this movie. Like a lot of British sci-fi movies, this was well scripted, and especially well acted.

Our hero is naval officer Bill Masen (Howard Keel), who begins the movie in the hospital with his eyes bandaged, so he misses the spectacular light show caused by the meteors. He keeps his sight, while most of the rest of humanity are blinded. Masen saves little Susan (Janina Faye) from a train wreck. You guessed it, the train conductor couldn't see. While you have people stumbling around all over London, Masen and Susan head for France to find safety there.

Now, in case you are wondering, the Triffids seem to have been created by space spores linked to the meteor shower. Not only are they man-eaters, but they have mobility, too, and can disable their victims with a poisonous stinger. Hard to argue with that.

If you thought this was the entire plot, you'd be wrong. Cloistered away in a lighthouse are scientists Tom and Karen Goodwin (Kieron Moore, Janette Scott) who do battle with the Triffids when they start trashing the lighthouse. They are also seeking a means to defeat the killer plants.

Masen and Susan manage to make it to a safe haven, but it's Tom and Karen who save the day. Under attack by the Triffids, and almost out of running room (they escape to the top of the light house), they turn a hose on the Triffids that pours seawater on them. You guessed it again, the Triffids dissolve, and what's left of humanity is saved.

Recently I had a chance to meet the lovely Janina Faye at a sci-fi convention in New Jersey. We talked a little about *The Day of the Triffids,* and I asked about production issues on the film. I remember as a kid that the film seemed to take forever to come out. She indicated that there was some dissatisfaction with the ending, and the ending shown in the film was shot almost a year and a half after original production stopped.

Dangers from outer space have been a frequent theme in sci-fi yarns. Most of the time, we seem to find a way to save ourselves, and, of the films I have seen, this is the second example of water saving the day. (The other example is the 2002 film *Signs.*) *The Day of the Triffids* is a period gem that's convincingly presented and wonderfully entertaining. It was good enough to spawn a mini-series in 2009. For some reason the movie is not on TV all that often.

Dr. Strangelove or: How I Learned to Stop Worrying and Love the Bomb *and* Fail-Safe (American, 1964)

Both

In 1964, two films were released with a fairly similar story: *Dr. Strangelove,* a film about a nuclear holocaust, and *Fail-Safe,* a movie that showed the risks involved with nuclear weapons and poor relationships. Now, some may argue whether these are truly post-apocalyptic films, but the nuclear war aspect certainly helps make the case. In any event, a key difference is that *Dr. Strangelove* was basically a dark comedy. The film was directed by Stanley Kubrick, with a wonderful cast including Peter Sellers (in three roles), George C. Scott, Sterling Hayden, Keenan Wynn, and a very young James Earl Jones.

The cause of the nuclear catastrophe is a wacko general named Jack D. Ripper (Sterling Hayden)—certainly a message in that name—who believes the Russians are poisoning our water, so he authorizes a nuclear attack on the Russians. Both governments try to stop it, but to no avail. The film is funny thanks to the great talent of Peter Sellers. One classic line from the film has the Russian ambassador fighting with American generals who believe he is trying to steal secrets. At that point, the American president says, "Gentlemen, you can't fight in here! This is the War Room." George C. Scott's cavalier attitude about American casualties from a war with Russia is kind of funny in a very scary way. The film ends with Major "King" Kong (Slim Pickens) riding a nuclear bomb into a Russian city, followed by total nuclear war.

Fail-Safe is a far more sobering film that rubs your nose in the dangers of nuclear weapons. This time, it is not a wacky general that's the problem, but a series of technical glitches that enable American bombers to breach Soviet airspace. Despite the best attempts of both sides to stop the bombers, one gets through and takes out Moscow. The American president (Henry Fonda) makes the decision to drop a nuclear bomb on New York to appease the Russians and avoid total war. A very grim, but effective, film that completely reflects our fear of nuclear war. I still maintain that post-apocalyptic films are a reflection of our fears and a way to make them entertaining, or perhaps less threatening—a little like thrill rides at an amusement park.

Crack in the World (American, 1965)

For those of you who think mankind is likely to be the cause of the apocalypse, *Crack in the World* is the movie for you. Released in 1965

and staring Dana Andrews, Janette Scott, and Kieron Moore, the film shows how human folly can screw up the works. It's certainly not the best sci-fi flick out there, but the story is interesting, even if it is sometimes tedious and predictable.

If this one doesn't strike your fancy, you can't blame the cast. Dana Andrews has been in some really great films, including *The Best Years of Our Lives*. And how can you not like Kieron Moore, who saved the world from man-eating plants in *The Day of the Triffids* just a couple of years earlier? We start out innocently enough as Dr. Stephen Sorenson (Dana Andrews) attempts to tap geothermal energy from deep inside the Earth. Sounds like a good idea, right? But after drilling and drilling they can't penetrate the last part of the Earth's crust to get to the magma. So let's do what we always do when we have one of these problems: explode a nuclear device to clear the way. Makes sense to me; just think of the free energy we get out of this!

A minor problem emerges—minor if you are prone to understatement; they make a crack in the world. This crack appears to be trashing everything in its way as it spreads. The world appears doomed. So time for some "out of the box" thinking. If you're wondering where this leads, yup, time for another nuclear detonation to release the pressure and stop the crack. Seemed like a good idea at the time. Well, what this does is send the crack back in the direction of where it started. In the end, a huge chunk of earth is hurled into space, creating another moon, but it appears we are saved. While all this is going on, there is a love triangle between Dr. Stephen Sorenson (Dana Andrews) and Dr. Ted Rampion (Kieron Moore) for the affections of Dr. Maggie Sorenson (Janette Scott), who is Sorenson's wife. Not to worry, Stephen is dying anyway, so Ted gets the girl in the end. Not a particularly great film, but certainly the subject was new, and not without some value.

Planet of the Apes (American, 1968)

Probably the most spectacular post-apocalyptic film of the 1960s was *Planet of the Apes*. This film has spawned a franchise that continues

to this day. Originally released in April 1968, this film had several sequels, a TV show, and many remakes. However, in my opinion, none
can compare to the first. Sure, some of the special effects got better, but
the script and a masterful job by Charlton Heston made this film the
gold standard.

While the film is so novel and engaging, it does, after all, take us
back to our post-apocalyptic roots. This is essentially a story about
nuclear war and its consequences. George Taylor (Charlton Heston),
along with two shipmates, crash-lands on a planet after being in deep
hibernation for over 2,000 years. They set out to explore their new
world, and discover humans that are mute, and rather backward. In
fact, they are seen as a nuisance by the planet's other inhabitants, and
are routinely rounded up and destroyed.

Taylor is with his buddies watching the humans forage when he
hears a loud noise, and the utter shock on his face when he sees apes
riding horses and holding guns is priceless. A fantastic scene! Taylor
loses his friends, gets injured, and is captured by the apes. Because the
injured Taylor can't talk, the apes think he is a typical human. When he
gets his voice back, the ape world freaks out!

Even though Taylor is aided by two apes, Cornelius (Roddy McDow-
ell) and Zira (Kim Hunter), it's clear the ape leaders are no fans of Taylor, and would like to see him disposed of. You get the feeling that they
know something most apes don't.

Taylor escapes, and heads for what the apes call "The Forbidden
Zone," and tangles with Dr. Zaius (Maurice Evans). Along the way,
Zaius warns Taylor about his attempt to find his destiny, telling him
"you may not like what you find." Taylor ignores him and heads off into
the sunset. He rides into the Forbidden Zone on horseback, and the
viewer sees a pointy shadow on the sand. A moment later Taylor is horrified by what he sees: the upper portion of the Statue of Liberty! Taylor
realizes he is on Earth, and that the human race was nearly destroyed in
a nuclear war. He damns his ancestors to hell in a very powerful ending
scene.

In this truly impressive film, once again, nukes play the key role in
our demise. That theme would continue in the years ahead, but to quote
Dylan, "The Times They are a Changin'."

Night of the Living Dead (American, 1968)

In October 1968, a relatively low budget film was released with a cast of mostly unknown actors that would have a profound effect on science fiction movies. That film was *Night of the Living Dead*. I saw the film for the first time at a midnight showing in the summer of 1971 at the Waverly Theater in Greenwich Village. It was a packed house that night, and the movie scared the hell out of me. I can still remember hearing a young woman's voice shouting out "this is sick" when a bunch of ghouls in the movie started to eat the remains of two characters in the film. For some reason, that brought about some laughter in our audience. Notice I called them ghouls, but now everybody considers them zombies. I ran into George A. Romero, one of the creators and the director of the film, a few years ago at a sci-fi convention, and he said he never used the word zombie in the film. That is true, but *Night of the Living Dead* has to be considered the first modern zombie movie.

I'm not going into a specific list of zombie movies, but the idea has been around for many years. In 1932, Bela Lugosi headlined the film *White Zombie,* where the bad guy turns people into zombies with some voodoo. In his book *Zombie Movies: The Ultimate Guide* (2008), Glenn Kay discusses Karloff's role as a zombie in the film *The Walking Dead* (1936). Kay describes Karloff as a sympathetic figure, who really doesn't want to kill. Interestingly, Kay states that this film includes the first time a zombie is killed by a bullet to the head. I have been a Karloff fan all my life, but oddly enough, this is not a film I have ever seen. Another oldie but goodie is a film called *I Walked with a Zombie*, released in 1943. This is another one that got by me, but here again, the film takes place in the Caribbean and voodoo is part of the story.

Another voodoo-related zombie flick, and released more recently, was the Hammer Film *The Plague of the Zombies* (1966). While I have never seen this flick, IMDb indicates that when a mysterious outbreak kills off young minors, voodoo is suspected of bringing the dead back to life. As more of a black magic–type flick, it didn't seem to fit the post-apocalyptic genre.

You can make a case that a lot of old films were zombie-like in their content. Ghoul or zombie, what's the difference, after all? But when you talk about *Night of the Living Dead,* you're talking about something special. This wasn't a story about some wacko guy in Haiti turning people into zombies every now and then with voodoo. This film presents a mass-scale event that threatens all of humanity. While it isn't totally clear what caused the dead to rise up, one scientist suggests it's from radioactive contamination from a space probe. So now we begin to move away from nuclear war as the possible end of humanity. Bottom line: stay away from dead guys.

The film starts out with Barbara (Judith O'Dea) and Johnny (Russell Streiner) paying their respects to a family member at a cemetery when they are attacked by "Zombie Number One" (Bill Hinzman). Zombie Number One would become part of zombie folklore, as Hinzman's character was the first zombie to appear in the film. Barbara escapes to a farmhouse where she hooks up with Ben (Duane Jones), who tries to help her survive the apocalypse. Jones is probably one of the first African-Americans to have a leading role in a sci-fi flick.

Ben tries to shore up the house, and eventually they find out there are others in it. They devise a plan to leave the place, but the plan goes bad and two of them end up as "crispy critters" for the zombies to munch on. Eventually, the place is overrun by zombies, and things go from bad to worse. Some rather horrific scenes unfold, including a man and woman getting killed by their own daughter, and Barbara getting dragged from the house by the zombie horde, which includes her brother. I found that to be a fairly intense part of the film. Ben survives by hiding in the basement, only to be shot in the head the next morning by "zombie hunters." A depressing end, but powerful!

Over the years, I have had a chance to meet most of the surviving members of the cast at various sci-fi conventions. I can even recall dragging my kids to some of these events to meet Bill Hinzman and some of the others. But this was a milestone film that I believe set the stage for a cottage industry and genre of films with considerable staying power. This film has spawned dozens of other films, and even a couple of TV shows. For the most part, all the zombie characterizations you see in other movies have come from this film.

As I have said earlier, perhaps these films make our fears about the world less threatening, or in some strange way serve as a release for these fears. We started the decade with the horrible consequences of nuclear war, and end it with the first stage of a zombie apocalypse. Maybe all this means is that there is more than one thing to be afraid of, and films over the next 40 years make a convincing case for that. At a deeper level, perhaps these films represent a fatalism or pessimism about the future. While it could be the neurosis of an aging baby boomer, the future seems less predictable now and more uncertain than at any point in my lifetime. Who says there are no zombies out there!

Chapter Four: The 1970s

The Andromeda Strain (American, 1971)

While there have certainly been decent post-apocalyptic flicks in the 1970s, and the 1980s, too, I was far less impressed with the flicks from this period. Perhaps that was the effect of disco music. The *Planet of the Apes* franchise continued to crank out installments during this period, and some were rather good, but I think readers have already gotten the idea of what to expect there. Other films were basically ho-hum, but there were some goodies.

One of those goodies was *The Andromeda Strain*, released in 1971, and based on a Michael Crichton novel. For some reason, this is a film I have seen only twice: first when it was originally released, and once on TV. I remember being impressed with the movie, which had a good cast of 1970s actors including James Olsen, Arthur Hill, and David Wayne. The film was directed by the legendary Robert Wise, who directed some great films including *West Side Story*, *The Sound of Music*, *The Day the*

Earth Stood Still, and *Run Silent, Run Deep*. He also directed an outstanding little move called *The Set-Up*, which is a film about corruption in boxing. With a solid cast and Robert Wise as your director, how can you lose?

OK, the bad news is a satellite (Scoop 7) returns to Earth and kills just about everybody in a small town in New Mexico. For some reason, an old man and a baby are the only two survivors. The good news is that the government has a bunch of really smart guys who are part of a team designed to handle these types of emergencies. They even have a cool super-high-tech research facility in Nevada.

In fairly short order, the scientists figure out that whatever is killing people is transmitted in the air, and kills just about anything almost instantly. And if you think you are safe flying way above it, think again. One cool sequence in the film shows a fighter pilot's mouthpiece and air hose disintegrate from exposure, causing the pilot to crash.

While I didn't recall why the baby survived, according to Wikipedia, the baby cried so much that he was perpetually hyperventilated, making his blood too alkaline for the virus. The old man escaped harm because he had been drinking Sterno. There is something to be said for heavy drinking during the apocalypse. In any case, the scientists figure out this stuff is some kind of life form that is dangerous to us, and a decision is made to nuke it. Ever notice how many times we try nuking stuff in the movies and it never seems to work? Well, this time they conclude not only will the bomb not work, but it will spread the virus, too. In the nick of time, the scientists stop the nuke and instead decide to let alkaline rain wash it away into the sea.

This was a well-done film that sets the stage for films that focus on viruses and germs as a threat to humanity, as well as stuff from outer space.

The Crazies (American, 1972)

A couple of years later, in 1972, George Romero came out with one of his cult classics, *The Crazies*. This film tells the story of a biological weapon that, thanks to poor handling and incompetence, infects a small town in Pennsylvania. This theme will become more popular in the coming years, and, as a matter of fact, will still be showing up 40 years later in films like *Parts Per Billion* (2014). *The Crazies* is a great Romero film that has a little of everything, including self-immolation, incest, redneck uprisings, and military mismanagement. There are aspects of the film that are similar to *The Andromeda Strain,* but more so to the film *Outbreak* (1995), which also had a small town potentially being wiped out to prevent additional infection.

We start out innocently enough with two lovers (who are basically our heroes), Judy (Lane Carroll) and David (Will MacMillian), enjoying each other's company. Suddenly, they both get calls—she is a nurse and he is a volunteer fireman—about a fire and some injuries. Things go downhill from there.

To make a long story short, a biological weapon ends up in the water supply of the town and starts infecting people. The good news is that you go crazy if infected, while the bad news results in death. Nice choice. Soon after the problem is detected, U.S. military personnel start showing up to gain control of the situation. Reflecting the time period the film was made, you can see surprise from local police when the man in charge is African-American, Colonel Peckem (Lloyd Hollar). His job is to contain the virus by sealing off the town, and finding out who is infected. Of course, if things get really bad, an American bomber is flying overhead to drop a nuke, if necessary. How well do you think that will work out!

The town folks are not all that happy about being rounded up and sent to the high school, so some of them resist and try to escape. Judy and David, with some help from a local doctor, escape with a couple of other people. And some of the local rednecks decide to take up arms and shoot it out with the soldiers who are running around in white suits and gas masks.

Meanwhile, the military brings in one of the scientists involved in the development of the weapon to find a cure. While he is working on that, the army is trying to contain the infected, using the local school gym, of course. Judy, David, and their group are still trying to get out. One of their little group is a teenage girl who appears to be already infected. She kind of laughs at everything, and has the appearance of having dropped some bad acid at Woodstock. Her father starts to get infected, too. How do I know this? Well, he tries to have sex with his daughter. That pretty much does it for me. David's friend, Clank (Harold Wayne Jones), also starts to go wacko, and starts shooting people. But in the end, he does try to help Judy and David escape.

George Romero isn't a guy who appears to like happy endings. When our scientist finds a cure, he ends up getting pushed down the stairs, dropping the stuff during the chaos at the school. Well, so much for the future of humanity. Judy ends up being infected, and also manages to get shot by the soldiers. David, who appears to be immune, is taken into custody just as a doctor says if only they could find someone immune to develop a cure from. David just looks briefly at the colonel, who is now being sent off to another town to fight the same problem. While this isn't going to make it to the top of the post-apocalyptic film list, it is a fun flick to watch. And if the early nuke movies were a warning about the dangers of messing around with nuclear weapons, the message here is clear about biological weapons, as well!

The Omega Man (American, 1971)

In the early 1970s, Charlton Heston, one of my favorite actors, appeared in two major post-apocalyptic films. The first, released in 1971, was *The Omega Man*, which was based on the Richard Matheson novel *I Am Legend*. Now, I love post-apocalyptic films, and I love Charlton Heston, but I had a hard time getting into this one. Despite a good cast, the plot didn't click for me. Maybe the albino mutants weren't that convincing for me. As far as the plot goes, in the aftermath of a biological war, Dr. Robert Neville (Charlton Heston) is the last man on earth. Sound familiar? He avoids becoming a victim by developing some kind of vaccine that makes him immune.

The survivors are zombie vampire types who are sensitive to light, but are also wacko enough to want to take out Neville, since he is one of those terrible scientists who, after all, created this mess. Neville eventually hooks up with a woman, Lisa (Rosalind Cash). He starts to treat her as she is infected with the disease. Unfortunately, he is not successful, and he ends up getting speared by a mutant and dies the next day. For some reason, I enjoyed the film *The Last Man on Earth* (1964), also based on the *I Am Legend* novel, better.

Soylent Green (American, 1973)

In 1973, Charlton Heston once again appeared in a post-apocalyptic film, *Soylent Green*. This is a great film with an incredible cast that also includes Edward G. Robinson, Chuck Connors, Joseph Cotton, Brock Peters, Leigh Taylor-Young, and the ever-present Whit Bissell. This is an important film because it focuses on man's proclivity for trashing his environment. In fact, this is probably the first major flick about man's negative impact on the environment (excluding nuclear war, of course). Eco-terrorists have to love this one. Over-industrialization and global warming leave the world in a mess. Cities are dramatically over-crowded, with millions of homeless people wandering the streets. Just about everything, especially food, is in short supply. What would a post-apocalyptic film be without an evil corporation profiting off the misery of the huddled masses? In this case, that is the Soylent Corporation.

This company supplies food to those huddled masses through a product called Soylent Green. Forget the ham and eggs; this stuff is some kind of nutritious plankton that is rationed out to people. Our heroes in this flick are Detective Thorn (Charlton Heston) and police analyst Sol Roth (Edward G. Robinson). The interaction between Thorn and Roth really helps make this movie. In one of the best scenes, the two are enjoying a few scraps of food Thorn stole from a rich guy's apartment, and you really feel their elation and depression at the same time. Remember, real beef is not to be had in this world, which is basically stuck munching on Soylent Green all the time.

As Thorn investigates the murder of a wealthy man, he discovers a document that ties the victim to the Soylent Corporation. Along the way, Thorn questions the very attractive Shiri (Leigh Taylor-Young), the wealthy man's mistress. Who could resist Charlton Heston? So the two develop a relationship of their own. He learns the rich guy was troubled before he was killed, and pushes forward with the investigation. Seems like some folks don't like where this is going, so Thorn is told to back off. Now, does anybody think that Thorn is going to back off? You got it, and after pissing enough people off, they try to have him assassinated.

Meanwhile back at the ranch, Sol Roth investigates the reports he got from Thorn, and finds there is something funny about Soylent Green. Sometimes reading the packaging isn't enough! Roth now knows it's probably made from human remains, and decides to opt out at a government suicide clinic. I thought this scene was touching, and wonderfully played by Robinson. While Thorn tries to stop it, he is too late, but Roth asks him to let the world know the truth.

Thorn investigates, and makes it to a garbage disposal plant where he sees human remains converted to Soylent Green. He comes back with the truth and gets injured in a fight with one of the conspirators. However, he calls the police station and tells his boss, Chief Hatcher (Brock Peters), to tell the world that Soylent Green is dead people. I have always enjoyed this film because it is a great story that was told by the actors and not special effects. As I mentioned earlier, this film is also the first major installment in apocalyptic films about man's impact on the environment.

The Last Wave (Australian, 1977)

Without the Wikipedia apocalyptic list I would never have known about the film *The Last Wave*, released in 1977. After watching it, I'm not even sure it is a post-apocalyptic film in the traditional sense, but the ending suggests the possibility. The film stars Richard Chamberlain, king of the made-for-TV movies, and wasn't he great in *Shogun*?

In this flick, Chamberlain is a lawyer, David Burton, assigned to defend a group of Aborigines accused of murder. It appears that Burton has been plagued by weird dreams and premonitions his entire life, which makes his involvement with the Aborigines more intense because of the importance of dreams in their culture. While he'd forgotten about some of his childhood dreams, his father reminds him that a month before his mother's death he had dreams about it, and actually predicted the way she would die. The story takes place in Australia, which has been experiencing some strange and very wet weather. This gives the film a very bleak and depressing feel.

As Burton digs into the defense of his clients, his dreams become more intense, and he comes to feel the murder was a killing by tribal curse. It also seems he comes to see the bad weather as the sign of an impending apocalypse. He eventually befriends one of the Aborigines, who warns him about the dangers of getting involved in their world. Part of this danger resides in a tribal priest whom he battles in an underground tunnel. Burton eventually returns to the surface. When he reaches it, he falls to his knees and for an instant you see a giant tidal wave that can wash away Australia, and perhaps the rest of the world, too. It appears only to be a premonition, but given his history, I'd head for high ground. If you are a post-apocalyptic purist, you may want to pass on this one, since it's only in the final scene you really get a sense for what might happen.

Dawn of the Dead (American, 1978)

OK, now it's time to go back to the zombies. In 1978, the cult classic *Dawn of the Dead* was released. George Romero did a couple of films after *Night of the Living Dead*, but *Dawn of the Dead* was another milestone for him. The film tells an interesting story, has a good cast, and even the artwork for the film is really cool; a movie poster showing a mutilated human head coming up over the horizon says it all.

While I did enjoy the film, at the risk of committing post-apocalyptic heresy, I actually enjoyed the 2004 remake better. So much for political correctness! In any case, as far as the plot goes, some kind of weird phenomenon causes people to turn into flesh-eating zombies; so what else is new! Of course, the military and the government can't stop it. So after battling zombies and a wacko SWAT team, four survivors—Stephen, Peter, Roger, and Francine—leave the city and end up at an abandoned shopping mall. They make this their home, and take out zombie squatters in the mall. So far, so good! However, one of them carelessly gets bitten by a zombie, and as they prepare to leave the mall things take a turn for the worse.

Now, when was the last time a biker gang showed up in a movie and things got better? For some reason one of the survivors starts a gun battle with the bikers, gets shot, and ends up a zombie himself. The two remaining survivors get into a helicopter and fly off into the zombie sunset. Not quite the romantic ending you find in the old westerns, but this is what you get in the zombie apocalypse.

A Boy and His Dog (American 1975)

I'm a big Don Johnson fan, but the movie *A Boy and His Dog*, released in 1975, did very little for me. The film was set 50 years into the future (2024), and those lovable rascals in charge once again destroyed the world with nuclear war. From a very bleak landscape emerge our hero, Vic (Don Johnson), and his dog, Blood, with whom he communicates telepathically. Blood's keen sense of smell helps them find food and females, which is all Vic appears to want.

After finding a woman killed by marauding bandits out in the wasteland, the pair move on, steal some food from another group of lowlifes, and find their way to a camp that has moving pictures (actually soft porn), but Vic and Blood don't care. Blood manages to find a woman in what appears to be an underground tunnel or storage dump. Vic meets the seductive Quilla (Susanne Benton), and fights off some other creeps to keep her.

While Vic thinks he has control over the poor, defenseless Quilla, she is actually setting a trap for him. It seems she lives in an underground community that can no longer reproduce because they have lived underground for too long. Lou Craddock (played by none other than Jason Robards) heads the community, and they are always out looking for "new blood" to help them out of a jam. The good news is they will use the virile Vic to help with their reproduction problems; the bad news is they will kill him when they are finished.

Despite the odds, Vic gets away with a little help from Quilla, and the two manage to get to the surface. Once there, Vic looks for Blood, and fears he has lost him because he was gone too long. He finds poor Blood, injured and starving, and wonders about his next move. Quilla urges Vic to leave Blood because he is too far gone. The screen fades to black, and the next thing you know, Blood had a good meal, and the two are headed back into the wasteland. Lesson number one: don't try to come between a boy and his dog, as you may end up on the menu. This was a rather forgettable and sometimes tedious movie, which was the fault of the script and not the cast.

Logan's Run (American, 1976)

Perhaps one of the most well-known 1970s post-apocalyptic films is *Logan's Run*, released in 1976. Oddly, this is one of those films I saw for the first time very recently. It has a strong cast, including Michael York as Logan, Richard Jordan as Francis, Jenny Agutter as Jessica, and a very young Farrah Fawcett as Holly. The story begins in 2274, after the world has been devastated by over-population and pollution. People live in a glass-domed city that reminds me a lot of EPCOT at Disney World: very clean, neat, and relaxed, and not too much work to do. But there's one problem—and this isn't going to go over well with you aging baby boomers out there—at age 30 you are out of there. Basically, you are terminated, which helps them control the population. Remember, the "Woodstock generation" said never trust anyone over 30—well, they just took it a little further.

Now, they do offer a chance at renewal for those who reach 30 in a ceremony called the Carousel. However, this is all for show, as nobody ever makes it to renewal. Our hero is Logan, who is a "sandman," which is someone who hunts down and kills people who decide to run (runners) to try to save their lives rather than participate in the Carousel. Basically a sandman is a terminator. Along the way, Logan picks up a girlfriend, Jessica, who may have involvement in an underground group that helps runners find safety in a place called Sanctuary, which is in the outside world.

Logan is asked to infiltrate this group and destroy it. The bad news is that his cover story includes his life clock being accelerated to the age of a runner. Eventually, Logan feels he is screwed, and does become a runner, but is relentlessly pursued by his friend, Francis. After enduring many hardships on the outside, including traveling through a decaying Washington, DC, he and Jessica come across the "old man" (Peter Ustinov). They are amazed at seeing someone so old still alive. After finally killing Francis, Logan decides to take the "old man" back to show the others people can live beyond thirty. And while the world used to be a mess, their trip shows a much better place now.

Logan returns and manages to overload and destroy the computer, opening the seals to the outside world. As the people escape the city, they, too, see and are amazed by the "old man" and realize life can last much longer than thirty years. *Logan's Run* is an entertaining film, and while it may not be representative of most post-apocalyptic films, it is worth watching.

Mad Max (Australian, 1979)

We close out the 1970s with the low-budget Australian film *Mad Max* (1979), which is perhaps a little less noteworthy. Most Americans would consider this a "little movie," but it has generated a cult following, and is still generating sequels.

Society appears to be on the verge of collapse (it's not totally clear why), but it does in part relate to energy and other basic need shortages. The bad news is that biker gangs—yup, we are back to biker gangs—control the roads and threaten society. Our hero is Max (Mel Gibson), who is kind of a highway patrolman who chases down the wacko road gangs.

A character called Nightrider, who, after killing a young cop, tries to escape the police in a suicidal car chase, tests Max. Max will have none of this, and outmaneuvers Nightrider, who dies in a fiery car crash. Nightrider's biker gang goes on a rampage, raping a young woman, trashing a town, and killing another cop, who was a friend of our hero, Max. Max considers pulling out of the force, but takes a trip with his wife, Jessie (Joanne Samuel), and their child.

While on vacation, the biker gang catches up with Max and his family, and kills his wife and child. Max, not surprisingly, loses it, and starts eliminating the gang members. He rams and ambushes them, and when he finds one of the leaders, he handcuffs him to a car and sets a timer to blow him up, but in an act of compassion leaves him a hacksaw, so the gang leader has a choice to cut his leg off instead of getting blown up. You are never sure about what choice he made, but an explosion says he may not have been fast enough with the saw. Max eventually drives off into the sunset—or should I say the Outback—never to return. Well, at least not until the sequel a couple of years later.

Chapter Five: The 1980s

Night of the Comet (American, 1984)

The decade of the 1980s was a crazy time in America, a time of chaos and excesses that continue to shape our world today. Some of the things we saw way back when included leveraged buyouts, hostile takeovers, MTV, the AIDS virus, Ronald Reagan becoming president, the Berlin Wall taken down, and Pan Am flight 103 being bombed by terrorists. In the world of movies, we saw some great flicks, including *Raging Bull*, *Wall Street*, *E.T.*, *Ghostbusters*, *Platoon*, and *Raiders of the Lost Ark*.

However, when we come to post-apocalyptic films it's kind of a mixed bag: some very good, some not so good! And some had me thinking, *Why did I like that movie the first time I saw it?* In that category is *Night of the Comet* (1984), otherwise known as the Valley Girls Meet the End of the World. Some consider this a cult film; I found it annoying the last time I saw it. The plot explores the impact of the Earth going through a comet's tail, and, like in *The Day of the Triffids*, people go out and watch the event. Bad idea! By the next morning everybody who watched is turned into dust or a zombie. Not much of a choice here.

Of course, there are some survivors, including Reggie Belmont (Catherine Mary Stewart), who is too busy playing video games to see the comet, and her kid sister Samantha (Kelli Mahoney), who got punched out by her stepmother. The girls manage to hook up with another survivor, Hector Gomez (Robert Beltran). They stay together for a bit, but Hector leaves to find his family. The girls decide to do what "valley girls" do: go shopping at the mall. After a fight with some zombies, the girls are eventually rescued by some scientists. The scientists are a dead end (kind of bad guys), but Reggie rescues a boy and girl who would have been used by the scientists in their search for a cure, and hooks up with Hector again. Sam looks to be the odd person out, but she meets up with Danny and drives off into the sunset. Now, this film can be funny at times, and the plot is fairly interesting, but, like me, I don't think it aged well.

Land of Doom (American, 1986)

Another rather forgettable 1980s flick was *Land of Doom*, released in 1986. This was kind of a low budget *Mad Max/Road Warrior* rip-off that had a female Rambo-type character called Harmony (Deborah Rennard) as the lead. She may have listened to Helen Reddy's *I Am Woman* too many times, because she comes off as a little bit too hostile in the beginning. But who can blame her? The world has been destroyed by nuclear war, and a bunch of guys called "raiders" are running around on motorbikes trying to trash what's left.

She runs into a guy named Anderson (Garrick Dowhen) who has been injured in a battle with the raiders. Reluctantly, she allows him to go with her, and on their way out of a trashed village, they stop and visit with a guy who offers them some human stew. Politely, they refuse, and after beating on their host a little, they march on. The music and sets are definitely 1980s, and I'm sure parts of it were filmed at Studio 54.

After witnessing the raiders trashing yet another village, they steal a motorbike and try to get away. On route, they help a guy named Orland

(Akut Duz) who is being attacked by some junkyard dogs. He goes with them for a while, and when Harmony and Anderson are captured by the raiders, Orland follows them. To make a long story short, Orland helps them escape the raiders, and Harmony warms up to Anderson. However, as the film ends, the three are once again chased by the leader of the raiders, and they run off into the post-apocalyptic sunset. Another one that won't make your can't-miss film list.

Virus *or* Day of Resurrection (Japanese, 1980)

Probably a more obscure film that was released in 1980 was *Virus*, also known as *Day of Resurrection*. While this was a Japanese film, the cast was a virtual who's who among aging American actors, including Glenn Ford, Chick Connors, George Kennedy, Robert Vaughn, Bo Swenson, Henry Silva, and Edward James Olmos. If you thought we were finished with virus movies after the *Andromeda Strain*, you were wrong. It seems like those loveable government scientists are at it again, creating a deadly virus, which of course has no cure.

It almost falls into the wrong hands, but the government gets it back. However, virus MM88, affectionately known as the Italian Flu, spreads throughout the world and is killing people at an alarming rate. American President Richardson (Glenn Ford) doesn't have a clue, but wants the problem fixed. Good luck with that!

It seems like the only safe place to be is in Antarctica, and a small group of survivors—mostly men with just a few women—hang out there. Eventually many of the survivors get on an icebreaker ship in an effort to survive. Now I'm not going to complain about a virus that practically destroys humanity, but do we really need the nuclear war treatment, too? It seems that some earthquakes trigger nuclear defense systems, which our motley crew tries to stop, but they fail.

The good news is that a vaccine is invented along the way, so the folks who are left will be protected. There is an emerging love affair between Marit (Olivia Hussey) and Dr. Yamaguchi (Sonny Chiba), who was one of the guys sent to stop the nuclear launch. Well, we saw how well that went! Somehow, he manages to find the survivors and is reunited with Marit. She takes him back even though he looks like a homeless guy from the West Village. This is a rather confused film and, from my perspective, rather forgettable—and I actually saw it recently.

The Road Warrior (Australian, 1981)

I do not intend to go into many sequels, since we have been there and done that, but I did want to mention *The Road Warrior*, released in 1981. This is the second chapter in the Mad Max saga, and stars Mel Gibson as Max. This is set a couple years after the events of the first film and our hero, Max, is trying to help a band of survivors living in a gasoline refinery to defend themselves from barbarian road warriors trying to get the gas. Of course, Max comes through, but he ends up alone looking for new adventures. I actually liked this film better than the first one; a great script and a strong cast made this film come alive for me. Definitely post-apocalyptic honorable mention!

Warlords of the 21st Century (New Zealand/American, 1982)

On the other end of the spectrum is *Warlords of the 21st Century* (AKA *Battletruck*), released in 1982. This is a highly forgettable film (and I saw it relatively recently on YouTube) that is another low budget rip-off of the Mad *Max/Road Warrior* films. The story begins after World War III as order breaks down and road gangs terrorize the countryside looking for gas. Sound familiar? The worst of the lot is a guy named Straker

(Michael Wainwright) who has a militarized 18-wheeler that he uses to subjugate the local populations.

Straker and company find a large supply of diesel fuel in a remote area and decide to make that their base camp. Straker has a daughter named Corlie (Anne McEnroe), who seems to have a problem with her father's leadership style. When he orders her to kill the former owners of the diesel fuel, she refuses and runs away. She hooks up with our hero, Hunter (Michael Beck), who tries to hide her from "daddy dearest."

There are lots of chase scenes involving trucks and motorcycles—cheap footage, I guess. Nevertheless, Dad gets Corlie back, but Hunter sets a trap for Straker and his nasty truck with the help of some of the good locals. Hunter gets the girl, trashes the truck, and kills the dad, and, after all that, literally rides off into the post-apocalyptic landscape on a horse. This is one you might want to pass on!

The Aftermath (American, 1982)

Another one of those less-than-noteworthy films is the 1982 flick *The Aftermath*. This is a film I only saw once, and I think that will do it. Two of three astronauts return to earth only to find the world has been destroyed by nuclear war. Since they crash-land near LA, I'm not sure how they can tell anything is wrong. Well, it seems like some post-apocalyptic wacko named Cutter and his outlaw gang are in charge. Cutter's mission: get drunk, get women, and kill others. Simple plans always work best!

Of course, when the astronauts return to earth, they must also deal with some mutants. I'm not sure how long they were in space, but the world sure went to hell by the time they returned. Probably the best part of the film is an appearance by Forrest J. Ackerman as a museum curator, and the caretaker for a little boy who was all alone. Forrest is the well-known originator of *Famous Monsters of Filmland*, a classy monster magazine that started in 1958. In case you haven't guessed it, I have been a collector of that magazine since I was a kid.

One of our astronaut heroes, Newman (Steve Barkett), who reminds me of a refuge from a disco movie, ends up taking charge of the little boy, named Chris. Newman is a good surrogate dad, and teaches little Chris how to shoot. In post-apocalyptic times this is a critical skill. Well, I'm not sure what happens to the mutants, but Newman takes on Cutter's gang, and does fairly well until he gets killed, but little Chris takes care of Cutter. At the end, little Chris walks down the highway alone. You can put this one on your must-miss list!

The Terminator (American, 1984)

Probably the most significant post-apocalyptic film of the 1980s is *The Terminator* (1984). Directed by James Cameron, this is a true sci-fi classic that has a great script and a wonderful cast, including Arnold Schwarzenegger, Linda Hamilton, Michael Biehn, Paul Winfield, Lance Hennrikson, and a very young Bill Paxton as a not-so-tough tough guy.

The story takes place in 1984 Los Angeles, but really begins in the year 2029. A cyborg (the Terminator, played by Arnold Schwarzenegger) arrives in Los Angeles in 1984 to take out Sarah Connor (Linda Hamilton). Connor, it appears, will become the mother of John Connor. John Conner will lead the survivors who battle Skynet, an artificial intelligence network that dislikes people, and will create a nuclear holocaust to make that point. That is, unless the humans can stop Skynet. And the humans were doing OK, despite the rather bleak world in which they lived, so back in time comes the Terminator to get rid of Mama Connor, and by doing so, her son. This is to regain the advantage for the machines. Now, this cyborg is super strong and super smart, and almost impossible to kill. It sounds really bad, but the future sends some help in the form of Kyle Reese (Michael Biehn). Compared to the Terminator, Kyle is rather puny, but he is a resourceful guy. Besides, Sarah likes him, and they get really close.

Kyle helps Sarah escape the Terminator at a nightclub, but not after the Terminator basically trashes the place. After a high-speed chase, Sarah and Kyle end up in a police station. Safe at last! No, not really. Kyle tells his story to a police psychiatrist, who concludes he is a wacko. Well as it turns out, the joke is on them. The Terminator finds Sarah and Kyle, and kills a number of policemen in his assault on the station. However, our heroes escape to a motel, where they make bombs and plan to do battle with the Terminator. Of course, the Terminator again finds them.

After another chase, the Terminator gets his skin burned off by a pipe bomb, and Kyle gets wounded. Kyle uses his last bomb to try to destroy the Terminator, but he is also killed, and poor Sarah is left having to finish off the Terminator with a hydraulic press in a factory.

The end is rather poignant, as a pregnant Sarah travels around making tape recordings for her unborn son. She buys a picture of herself at a gas station, and years later her son, John, passes that picture off to Kyle before he goes back in time to help Sarah.

This was a big movie, and, not surprisingly, spawned a few sequels. However, fans would have to wait until 1991 for *The Terminator 2* to come out. At that time, I was a financial analyst involved in following film companies. And my recollection was that the huge cost of *Terminator 2* (I think over $100 million, according to IMDb) put a lot of financial pressure on the production company. Still, in the end, it was a very successful film, and I will discuss it more in the next chapter.

Escape from New York (American, 1981)

Another goodie from the 1980s is *Escape from New York* (1981). This is another classic, with some of my favorite actors. In addition to a great script, you get a chance to see Kurt Russell snarl his way through the movie as Snake Plissken. Kidding aside, this isn't your typical Kurt movie, but I enjoyed him nevertheless as Snake. Ernest Borgnine (an outstanding actor whom I was fortunate enough to meet briefly at a convention a couple of years before he died) also stars. Donald Pleasence, who plays the president, is one of those guys who often gets overlooked by the public. I can still remember how he gave a touching performance as an aging schoolmaster in a *Twilight Zone* episode. Add to this group Lee Van Cleef and Isaac Hayes, and you come up with a hell of a starting lineup.

As far as the storyline goes, we are told there is a massive increase in crime in America, and New York City has been turned into a maximum-security prison. At the time this film was made, there were probably some people who felt the city was already a maximum security prison. In any case, the president's plane is hijacked on the way back from a peace conference. When the plane crashes, he ends up in an escape pod within the NYC prison, which, of course, is surrounded by 50-foot walls. OK, what you do when the president is captured, and surrounded by criminals? Well, you send in another criminal to fetch him out. Enter Snake Plissken!

Now Snake is not all that excited about this job, even though he is going to get a pardon for attempting to rob the Federal Reserve. To give Snake a little extra motivation, the police commissioner (Lee Van Cleef) injects our hero with an explosive device that will blow him up in less than a day if he fails. Of course, since all the tunnels and bridges into the city are mined, Snake has to go in by glider, which lands on top of the World Trade Center.

The boss of the NYC penal colony is a guy called the Duke (Isaac Hayes). Now the Duke is trying to unify all the criminal gangs, and seems to want to use the president as a way to get them all off the island. Snake tries to rescue the president, but gets caught and is forced into a fight to the death with one of the Duke's brutes. Of course Snake wins the day, and he leads the president and a small group to the glider, which is unfortunately destroyed. But Cabbie (Ernest Borgnine), who helped Snake when he first arrived, tries to take them over the heavily mined 59th Street Bridge. Well, to make a long story short, while the others perish, Snake gets the president across the bridge to safety. The police commissioner neutralizes the explosive device in Snake, who refuses a job offer. Snake walks away destroying a tape with the president's comments that was to be presented to the American people. Snake substituted one of cabbie's old rock and roll tapes, and in the process made everyone look like fools.

Millennium (American, 1989)

The last film I'll comment on from the 1980s is *Millennium*, released in 1989. The plot is somewhat unusual in that the apocalypse happens in the future, and not the present day. It seems that pollution and over-population would end up producing a dead race that was barely hanging on. Things are so bad in the future that they steal dead people from our time to use them to help repopulate the earth at some point in the future. If you're wondering how, well, these people of the future could travel through time.

Our primary time traveler is a gal named Louise Baltimore (Cheryl Ladd) who has successfully nailed the punk rock look of the 1980s. It seems like the folks from the future are snatching bodies without any problem until our hero, Bill Smith (Kris Kristofferson), is called in to investigate a plane crash. Now, the trick to stealing bodies from the present is to not take anybody who would affect the future. So the only way to do this is to identify people who are destined to die, and steal them just before they die. The folks from the future like plane crashes because they are reliable sources of people. They want to avoid "timequakes" at all costs, since even their brief trips to the present could damage the timeline continuum.

Louise's mission is to divert Smith from his investigation, because he's getting close to figuring out some unusual things about this crash. Despite Louise's efforts to come on to Smith and keep him busy, Smith approaches Dr. Arnold Mayer (Daniel J. Travanti), a college professor, who has an idea about what's going on. Mayer figures this out because he managed to obtain a weapon from the future that was found in a 1963 plane crash. Well, as smart as Mayer is, he manages to kill himself with the weapon, which causes a massive timequake that threatens the very existence of the entire future world. The only thing to do to save the world is to send people they have snatched over the years into a more distant future and repopulate the earth. Since Smith has the hots for Louise, he goes into the new world with her as her world is destroyed. This is kind of an average flick that felt more like a made-for-TV movie. It's still entertaining, and the story is helped by a strong cast.

There are three other films I will comment on from the 1980s, but they are included in *Chapter 9: TV Apocalypse.* They are *Threads, The Day After,* and *Testament.* While *Testament* did have a brief theatrical release, it was originally designed for TV, and that's where I saw it. While television may not have been at the forefront of this subject, it does have a rich history that begins with *Twilight Zone* episodes and *Alas, Babylon* in 1960. If you look at TV today, it's full of made-for-TV apocalypses.

Chapter Six: The 1990s

Deep Impact (American, 1998)

✷✷✷✷

In the 1990s, post-apocalyptic films showed a little more variety than in the past. The 1980s reminded us that we still had to fear nuclear war, but now the 1990s demonstrated we had to add aliens and cosmic threats to our list. The asteroid or meteor threat probably caught the attention of people and moviemakers in the early 1980s, when Louis and Walter Alvarez came out with a new theory of what killed off the dinosaurs. They presented a case, ultimately confirmed by other scientists, that a giant meteor struck Earth about 65 million years ago and wiped out the dinosaurs. This new theory became popular, and it certainly got my attention. I can't say for certain if there is a direct correlation with this theory and a couple of key flicks from this period, but it sure looks like it.

Ok, so now we have to worry about giant rocks falling on our heads, as well as nuclear bombs. I haven't forgotten for one moment the 1951 film *When Worlds Collide* that was way ahead of its time. In any case, in the 1990s this new risk was made crystal clear in the films *Armageddon* and *Deep Impact*. Both came out in 1998, and both have strong casts and good scripts, but I was always a little more partial to *Deep Impact*—maybe because I've always liked Tea Leoni and Robert Duvall.

The storyline for *Deep Impact* is really great. It starts out with a couple of amateur kid astronomers figuring out that a comet is on a collision course with Earth. They pass this along to a teacher, who confirms the observation, but he is killed in a car crash as he tries to alert people. About a year later, a junior reporter, Jenny Lerner (Tea Leoni), is investigating the abrupt resignation of the Secretary of the Treasury, whom she thinks is having an affair with someone called Ellie.

Eventually, Jenny figures out that Ellie is really the acronym E.L.E., Extinction Level Event. The government isn't too happy with Jenny, who is threatening to spill the beans before President Beck (Morgan Freeman) wants to make an announcement. They work out a deal where Jenny backs off for a couple of days, and Jenny gets to be "numero uno" in the pressroom.

Jenny's career gets a big boost, but the end of the world is a hell of a time to ask for a promotion. Well, all is not lost yet, as the president announces a joint venture with the Russians to stop the comet. Of course to do this, they need some talented people, including aging astronaut Spurgeon Tanner (Robert Duvall), to help fly the mission… and, of course, a couple of nukes.

The problem is that they have to basically land on the comet and dig holes for the bombs so the blast can do its job. Unfortunately, the nukes don't work, and only manage to cut the comet into two very large pieces. The U.S. apparently has some really big caves in Missouri, and the government sets up a lottery to pick 800,000 people to join a pre-selected group of 200,000 in these caves. Talk about a high-stakes game.

All is not lost, thanks to the heroics of our astronauts. While one of the pieces causes massive coastal flooding and devastation to parts of America, Europe, and Africa, our space crew decides to go on a suicide mission to destroy the other piece. After tearful goodbyes to their families, they use their remaining nukes to destroy the second chunk of meteor. They succeed, and when the waters recede, President Beck reminds us that we should be grateful for a second chance, and urges the world to work together to rebuild. Now, who is going to say no to

Morgan Freeman? I thought it was a great movie, and the scene of Tea Leoni standing on the beach with her dad, waiting for the end, was especially powerful. This really personalized a catastrophic event.

Armageddon (American, 1998)

Also released in 1998 was the action-packed film *Armageddon*. Action star Bruce Willis is in top form as the leader of a group of wild and crazy roughnecks who are more interested in partying than saving the world. Now, Bruce Willis always kicks ass, so why should a little meteor be a big deal? In this film, Bruce is joined by a strong cast that includes Billy Bob Thornton, Steve Buscemi, Liv Tyler, Owen Wilson, and Ben Affleck.

After a meteor shower destroys the space station, astronomers observe a large asteroid, about the size of Texas, headed toward Earth. That's the good news! The bad news is that this will happen in less than three weeks and—you guessed it—mankind, along with everything else, will be wiped out. NASA decides to use nukes to blow the meteor apart and cause the pieces to bypass Earth. Sound familiar? By the way, you have to put the bombs 800 feet into the asteroid to make this plan work.

So, who ya gonna call? You got it, those hard-drinking over-partying roughnecks. At first glance these guys couldn't pass a physical that would allow them on an Amtrak train, let alone a spaceship. But NASA puts them into an accelerated training program; remember, this thing is going to hit in 18 days. Well, they somehow get in shape, and two ships head off to deal with the asteroid. While they succeed in blowing up the asteroid, a few mishaps (like hitting a gas pocket) cost them the lives of a few men, including Harry Stamper (Bruce Willis). The rest are hailed as heroes when they return. Part of the plot includes a romance between Harry's daughter, Grace (Liv Tyler), and roughneck A.J. (Ben Affleck). A.J. makes it back, and the two are married, showing pictures of the lost crew members at the event.

Terminator 2: Judgment Day (American, 1991)

While I don't want to spend a lot of time talking about sequels, I would be hard pressed not to cover *Terminator 2: Judgment Day.* This film, with a $100 million production budget, is just too big to ignore. The film includes the return of two key characters, Arnold Schwarzenegger as the Terminator, and Linda Hamilton as a very strung out, and sometimes annoying, Sarah Connor. We also have Robert Patrick as T-1000—the new and improved Terminator—and Edward Furlong as John Connor.

Once again, that pesky super-computer at Skynet is still trying to take out John Connor, the future head of the resistance. However, this time it tries to do it while he is a child. It sends the T-1000 (Robert Patrick), an advanced terminator that can change its shape into just about anything. He looks like some kind of liquid metal. But all is not lost, as the resistance reprograms an older model terminator to protect John. That's right, Arnold to the rescue! Just when the T-1000 is about to close in on John, Arnold saves him in an incredible motorcycle chase. A key difference between the first two *Terminator* movies is that the pace of the second is more intense, with lots of action and special effects. *Terminator 2* is an exciting flick, but kind of lacks the charm of the first, which got you a little closer to the characters.

Nevertheless, the world is in so much danger as Sarah concludes after she is busted out of a mental hospital that she must take out Skynet to stop the destruction of mankind. The best way to do this is to take out a Skynet engineer, Miles Bennett Dyson (Joe Morton), who is the guy responsible for the development of the technology that will be used against humans.

Sarah cannot kill Dyson, but gets him to support her efforts to stop Skynet. The police raid the house and shoot Dyson, but not before he blows up the lab, which supposedly houses all those terrible secrets that would be used by Skynet. However, none of this stops the T-1000 from trying to kill our heroes. In an epic battle of terminators, the T-1000 just about takes out the Terminator. But the Terminator ends up shooting the T-1000 into a vat of molten steel, and the T-1000 melts away. Victory at last—but not so fast. To prevent someone from redesigning another terminator, he, too, must go into the vat of molten metal. After some tearful goodbyes, he is lowered into the vat. That should be it for our story, but we know a couple more sequels will come out of this series. However, that's enough from me on the subject. It is enjoyable to watch, but even a good story can get stale if you tell it too many times.

Waterworld (American, 1995)

We've covered a couple of decent films, but now it's time to chat about *Waterworld*. Released in 1995 and starring Kevin Costner, Dennis Hopper, and Jeanne Tripplehorn, this is one I mostly had to force myself to watch. Although I had seen parts of it years ago, I could never stand to watch the whole thing. The sacrifices we must make when writing about post-apocalyptic films! For lack of a better description, it's kind of like *Road Warrior* without the road, and none of the excitement.

The story takes place, as best I can figure, a few hundred years in the future, after the polar ice caps have melted, leaving Waterworld. That's right, there's no land, and survivors are adrift in vessels best described as post-apocalyptic techno junk. Some of the survivors are bad guys, of course, especially Deacon (Dennis Hopper). Has Dennis Hopper ever been a good guy? One of the more interesting aspects of the film is that the bad guys are always smoking an endless supply of cigarettes. Perhaps that's why they are called "Smokers." Think about it. We're talking a few hundred years in the future, and everybody is on the water, so where did these cigarettes come from? I even saw some SPAM in one scene. I'll bet that was well past the expiration date, even for SPAM.

In any case, Mariner (Kevin Costner) is doing some trading at a watery outpost when they are attacked by Deacon's people, who are looking for a little girl who has a map tattooed on her back that supposedly shows where land can be found. Well, Mariner, the girl, and his future girlfriend escape on the open sea.

If the movie ended there we would have all been ahead of the game. But the plot thickens as Deacon's people capture the little girl, and he shows her off to his group that live on an old oil tanker. Yes, you guessed it, it's the Exxon Valdez. Mariner recues the little girl and they actually find land, which looks like a paradise from the Garden of Eden. They even have wild horses there. Now, I forgot to mention that Costner's character has gills so he can breathe under water. How this happens is unclear, but dry land doesn't suit him, so he takes a boat and drifts off into the sunset.

Independence Day (American, 1996)

Probably one of the biggest post-apocalyptic films of the 1990s, or general sci-fi for that matter, is *Independence Day*. Released in July 1996, with an all-star cast and a lot of fanfare, this film was a major box office success. From my perspective, it's kind of a high-tech remake of *War of the Worlds*, but wonderfully done. Interestingly, in the 1953 film, germs did in the aliens, perhaps a virus. In *Independence Day*, a computer virus helps bring about the demise of the aliens. In any case, the cast includes Will Smith, Bill Pullman, Jeff Goldblum, Mary McDonnell, Judd Hirsch, Randy Quaid, and Robert Loggia. I found it ironic that Robert Loggia practically launched his movie career fighting an alien spaceship in *The Lost Missile* in 1958, and almost 40 years later he was doing the same thing.

On July 2, 1996, a giant spaceship is detected orbiting the Earth. A number of smaller vessels, but still rather huge, are deployed over major cities around the world. At first, people don't know what to make of the situation, so we humans, being the good guys, attempt peaceful communication. A bad idea! A very smart cable guy, David Levinson (Jeff Goldblum), who is a former scientist, decodes an alien message and tells President Whitmore (Bill Pullman) their intentions are hostile. Some may be wondering how Levinson manages to talk to the president. Levinson's ex-wife works for the president, so he gets into the White House and spills the beans.

The problem is that there isn't much time between the warning and the alien attack. To make a long story short, attempts to communicate with the aliens are crushed, and many major American cities are trashed by the aliens. A really cool scene is when the president and his staff barely manage to take off in Airforce One as Washington, DC, is taken out.

But you know we aren't going to take any alien crap without teaching them a lesson. Bad idea number two! As we send out fighter jets to take out the aliens, we find their ships are protected by a force field, and, you guessed it, we get our asses kicked. However, one pilot, Captain Steven Hiller (Will Smith), manages to get an alien ship to crash-land after an intense chase. He sucker punches the alien and drags him off to Area 51, where it shortly becomes clear these guys have been here before.

After a nasty encounter with the alien at Area 51, President Whitmore decides to use nuclear weapons on the aliens. Bad idea number three. Didn't these guys watch the original *War of the Worlds* film from 1953? Nuclear bombs don't work on aliens! So now it looks like mankind is headed down the tubes. However, all is not lost. The cable guy figures out that we can get rid of the force fields with a computer virus. He and Captain Hiller use the old alien craft from Area 51, enter the mother ship, and disable the force fields. That's the good news, 'cause now our fighters can inflict damage to the alien ships. The bad news is that they run out of missiles, and are unable to take out an alien vessel. But our hero, Russell Casse (Randy Quaid), who insists that he once had been abducted by aliens, decides to fly a suicide mission into the alien ship, and does manage to take it out. While humanity was on the brink of being destroyed, we manage to come back and overcome those evil aliens. A well-done flick, that was very entertaining.

Judge Dredd (American, 1995)

In the less-than-stellar department, *Judge Dredd*, released in 1995, was a film I could have lived without. Despite a great cast that includes Sylvester "Rocky" Stallone, Diane Lane, Armand Assante, and Max Von

Sydow, the film never clicked for me. OK, so it was based on a comic book character, and had decent special effects, but it came off as dopey. We start off in the 22nd century, and Earth has become a vast wasteland, caused in part by pollution, with millions of people crowded into a small number of Mega-Cities. Things are so bad our planet is called the "cursed Earth." I felt a little cursed after watching it!

When you have thousands fighting over small condos and recycled food, which we are told is "good for the environment, and OK for you" (now that's an endorsement if I ever heard one), what can you expect? You got it, a breakdown of law and order, rioting, and rampant crime. We are told things are so dire that judges are hired to be judge, jury, and executioner of criminals. In other words, you get wacked if you get a parking ticket.

The toughest judge around is Judge Dredd (Sylvester Stallone). Would you expect anything else from the guy who played Rocky seven times? After blasting a few bad guys for parking tickets and otherwise inappropriate behavior, like shooting up the city, Dredd is accused of murdering a reporter. Of course, he is innocent, but they use DNA from his evil brother, Rico (Armand Assante), to convict him, and Dredd is sentenced to life imprisonment. He would have gotten the death penalty, but Chief Judge Fargo (Max Von Sydow) gets him off the hook as his final act as chief judge.

Dredd is sent to prison, but the aircraft crashes on its way to the prison, and Dredd is taken prisoner by cannibals. Yes, this movie has it all. They even have an experimental project called the Janus Project, which can produce genetically engineered judges. This isn't a bad idea, because Dredd's brother, Rico, is taking out judges like nobody's business. Rico is in league with the corrupt new Chief Judge Griffin (Jurgen Prochnow). Rico terrorizes the city and the Janus Project is approved. Meanwhile, back at the ranch, Dredd escapes from the cannibals and makes it back to Mega City, having realized what Rico and Griffin are trying to do. Dredd takes on Rico and, of course, takes him out in kind of a Rocky VII event. But Rico was at least nice enough to get rid of Griffin. The remaining judges are so impressed with Dredd they ask him to be chief judge. Dredd refuses, as he wants to always be a street judge. Could we expect any less from Rocky? As I said earlier, despite an impressive cast, this film did nothing for me.

Tycus (American, 1999)

Another 1990s film that wasn't a big hit for me was *Tycus*, released in 1999. The reason I decided to include it is that, like the first post-apocalyptic film, this was also about a comet that brings destruction to our planet. The second reason is I'm a Dennis Hopper fan, and still remember a number of his earlier films and his engaging performance in a *Twilight Zone* episode where he played a neo-Nazi leader.

The plot is somewhat predictable, as you have a gifted scientist, Peter Crawford (Dennis Hopper), who discovers a comet on a collision course with the moon. Of course, other scientists ignore him until it's too late. Crawford designs a plan for a nuclear rocket to intercept the comet. Been there, done that, and to no one's surprise it doesn't work. Not to fear, as Crawford has a backup plan that includes building a city underground to save a small number of people. While all this is happening, a reporter is trying to figure out what's really going on, but it's too late by the time he gets the real "scoop."

Crawford ends up going out to find his family, and is joined by the reporter, who wants to get his wife. They succeed and make their way back to the underground city, but their shelter has been discovered, and now lots of folks want in. Crawford insists they stay the course. However, at the last minute he is dragged out, but the others survive in the protected city. Meanwhile, out in the world, fragments from the moon trash the planet, and mostly destroy civilization. About 30 years later, when the world is in better shape, a small group sits on the side of a mountain listening to a young woman tell them what the world used to be like. This is basically a below average effort, but if you have about 90 minutes to waste this should do it.

Chapter Seven: Apocalypse in the New Millennium

or reasons that may seem obvious, post-apocalyptic films surged after the year 2000. We started the new millennium being scared out of our wits with fears of a massive computer system meltdown, often referred to as the Y2K problem. I think it was a software problem that would make information from the year 1900 indistinguishable from the year 2000, which would cause havoc in our data systems. Nothing happened, and it seems silly now, but on December 31, 1999, I was driving to New York City and a local radio DJ was interviewing a family who had moved into a bunker in preparation for the collapse that Y2K would bring. I wonder if they are still there.

In an effort to provide some balance, I have put zombie films in *Chapter 8: Modern Zombie Films*, rather than including them in this chapter. Someone out there is going to ask, how do you define modern zombie movies? My answer is films that were released after 2000. Once again, this is a subjective call, because zombie films are always linked to some kind of virus, but not all virus movies result in zombies. Some flicks are hard to call, but as I said, it is a subjective process.

The Day After Tomorrow (American, 2004)

My first entry into the non-zombie apocalypse category, and a must-see for all you global warming fans, is *The Day After Tomorrow* (2004). This is an extremely well done film with a great cast that includes Dennis Quaid (who I loved in *All the Right Stuff*) as paleoclimatologist Jack Hall. Other cast members included Jake Gyllenhaal (Sam Hall), Sela Ward (Dr. Lucy Hall), Ian Holm (Terry Rapson), and Jay O. Sanders (Frank Harris). This film is a wonderful blend of special effects and good storytelling that lets you get to know the characters in a personal way. Usually, you get one or the other in most sci-fi films these days. I also got a kick out of seeing my old building where I worked in lower Manhattan get washed away by a tidal wave.

We start our little adventure when Jack Hall and a couple of his buddies are drilling for ice core samples someplace up north. A huge part of the ice shelf breaks off while they are drilling. Hall reports his findings at a global warming conference in India. Jack lets people know that if we don't do something about global warming, eventually it will do something about us. The American vice president is there, acting like "the ugly American," and tells Jack to basically mind his business—after all, "our economic system" is every bit as fragile as the environment. Of course, nobody knows exactly when the environment is going to go down the tubes, but they should have gotten the message when Jack and Terry Rapson (Ian Holm) try to hail a cab in India and it's snowing.

Jack goes home, but soon severe weather is reported all over the world. Professor Rapson finds the ocean water temperature is dropping, and tornados are devastating Los Angeles. Jack's son, Sam, is in New York City on a class trip, and gets stuck there because of the crazy weather. Using Jack's climate model, he and Rapson conclude that the world will enter another ice age in a matter of days. Three super storms are reported over Canada, Scotland, and Siberia, freezing everything in their path. The world is facing catastrophe, and Americans start heading south to Mexico, entering illegally. Hall warns the president and vice president to evacuate the parts of the U.S. that still have a chance for people to get out. When asked what to do with the northern half of the country, Jack tells them it's too late for them, shocking the president and his cabinet.

Jack heads to New York to save his son, who is holed up at the main branch of the New York Public Library. Prior to his departure, Jack warns his son to stay put, since the temperature drop will be so sudden and severe that no one can survive. Of course, Sam warns people, but some leave the library and perish in the freezing temperatures. When Jack gets to his son, he calls the government, which is now headquartered in Mexico, for help. Jack and Sam are rescued, and we are reminded how nicely third world countries are treating those who are homeless because of the climate changes. This is a wonderful movie that made my post-apocalyptic top-ten list.

The Colony (Canadian, 2013)

The next film, *The Colony*, released in 2013, almost starts where *The Day After Tomorrow* leaves off. Here we are, more than 100 years later, and the world has gone into another ice age. It seems we have machines to protect us from climate change. Not surprisingly, the machines break down, and it snows for about a hundred years. Mankind has only one option: build underground tunnels to avoid the snow and cold.

Our little band is Colony 7, and is led by two former soldiers, Briggs (Laurence Fishburne) and Mason (Bill Paxton). Fishburne and Paxton are two of my favorite actors! Briggs is a stable guy and a good leader. Mason, on the other hand, is a little out there. Aside from dealing with the hardships of living in tunnels, with limited supplies, they all live in fear of any kind of infection. The common cold or flu can easily do them in. A recent flu outbreak killed 20 people, and the group established a quarantine system to protect them from those who are ill by isolating them. If you don't get better in a couple of days, you must leave the colony. You have a choice: to be shot or take the long walk. Our buddy,

Mason, isn't too keen on the long walk option because he thinks they will try to return, and he sees the sick as a drain on resources. So he just shoots them.

Briggs and Mason are at odds over this, but a distress call from Colony 5, with whom they have a support agreement, calls for action. Briggs takes a couple of his people to see what's happening. The good news is that they find a Colony 5 member alive. This person tells them they located another community that has fixed one of the weather machines and appears to be living outside, but are in need of seeds. The bad news is that the Colony 5 expedition didn't find the good-weather people, and instead brought back a group of cannibals who wiped out their colony.

Only one of the three from Colony 7 make it back alive, and even their leader, Briggs, is killed trying to stop the cannibals from following them. I'm sorry to report that they were unsuccessful, and the cannibals attack Colony 7, but our little group is up to the task, and destroys the cannibalistic group. Even Mason helps out by blowing himself and a number of cannibals up. Unfortunately, they also blow up their home, and, as the movie concludes, they start their trek to find the good-weather people. It's not a bad flick, but a little on the short side, and character development is a little weak. Still, it's a good airport movie!

Arctic Blast (Australian, 2010)

Another entry in the climate change apocalypse category is the film *Arctic Blast*, released in 2010. While it shares a similar cause with *The Day After Tomorrow* and *The Colony*, that's about all they share. Filmed in Tasmania, this flick flows more like a TV movie than something for theatrical release. It has the usual soap opera background and kind of cheesy special effects that cry out low budget TV movie. A bunch of kids are watching a solar eclipse, which somehow releases a cold blast of air that threatens mankind. For the record, according to the leading cast member, this is our fault, since pollution screwed up the ozone layer, and we are destined to become "popsicles."

Not to worry, scientist Jack Tate (Michael Shanks) will eventually save the day, despite marital problems with one of the blond women in the cast. Too many blonds make it a little hard to keep track of who is connected to whom. As the cold air blast starts freezing other parts of the world, people realize we are in a heap of trouble. Despite the fact that Jack is viewed as kind of a rogue by his superiors (remember this is like a TV movie, so what else could he be), he, nevertheless, helps them figure out a solution. After government weather balloons and rockets fail, Jack figures out to use some additional rockets that will help the ozone layer heal itself. Of course, Jack is also a good guy, too, and when a colleague needs some insulin to save her life, Jack leaves his teenage daughter to save the world as he heads to the drug store. Hey, I didn't write the script. The good news is that Jack gets the insulin, and his daughter saves mankind. After watching this movie, I'm not so sure that's a great idea. Despite some decent acting talent, this film came off as kind of amateurish and shallow. If you were doing some heavy drinking it might be worth a look; otherwise, I'd pass.

The Core (American, 2003)

We started with climate change, but that's not the only thing we have to worry about in the realm of post-apocalyptic films. What if the Earth's core stops spinning? Well, in 2003 you got a chance to find out all about it in the film *The Core*. Once the core stops spinning, all kinds of bad stuff happens; birds go wacko and attack people, powerful thunderstorms spring up, there's searing heat in places, and God help you if you have a pacemaker, because it isn't gonna work anymore.

So they get a bunch of smart people to figure out a way to save the Earth, and they do, and can you guess what that is? Well, there is only one thing you can do when the Earth's core stops spinning. You got it, use a couple of nukes to start it up again! I know mankind will be wiped out if they don't do this, but why do they always have to pull the nuke card in these movies? By the way, they need a special ship to drill into the Earth, called Virgil, and who do they get to pilot it? The people who, earlier in the movie, crash-landed the space shuttle! Makes sense to me.

Despite all kinds of challenges along the way, including the ship getting hit by giant diamonds and almost getting engulfed by molten lava, they make it to the core, but lose most of the crew along the way. They set off the nukes and, to my surprise, it actually works, and the last two crew members are saved. Now, they could've ended the story here, but I was surprised to find out that the government was working on a project—actually a weapon—to cause earthquakes and mayhem around the world. It seems those lovable idiots were the cause of the rotation stopping in the first place. This is a mildly entertaining film, which has a fairly impressive cast that includes Hilary Swank, Aaron Eckhart, Delroy Lindo, Stanley Tucci, and Bruce Greenwood. This is one to watch if you're waiting at an airport or on a plane, not one to stay up too late for.

2012 (American, 2009)

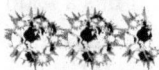

A few years later, in 2009, *2012* was released. Like the film *The Core*, this was about the Earth's core heating up, spelling disaster for humanity. However, this time it seems to be related to solar flares. This was also about the time people believed the end of the world was coming because the Mayan calendar said so! Actually, I think their calendar just ran out of space.

In any case, scientist Adrian Helmsley (Chiwetel Ejiofor) tells U.S. President Thomas Wilson (Danny Glover) that the Earth's core is going to do some bad things to our planet. President Wilson and other world leaders decide to build arks to save some of humanity. Something about this theme sounds familiar. But this film is far more complex than focusing just on the construction of a few arks. So we go to a down-on-his-luck writer, Jackson Curtis (John Cusack), whose wife dumped him for a plastic surgeon—sounds like a smart move to me. But the good news is he gets to spend quality time with his two kids, and even takes them to places like Yellowstone National Park. Some of you are thinking that's probably not a good place to be if the Earth's core is heating up, and you're right.

Of course, the army can't have civilians marching around Yellowstone, so they are removed from the park, but not before they meet Charlie Frost (Woody Harrelson), a kind of wacko environmentalist who hosts a radio show from the park. He sees the end coming, and eventually Jackson understands what's happening and rents a plane to save his family. He does it in dramatic fashion as a major earthquake drops LA into the sea—great special effects, but the jury still out about the loss of LA.

Now, with just a few arks built, you can imagine the ticket prices to get on one. By the way, no frequent flier miles are accepted. Jackson's employer, a Russian billionaire for whom Jackson chauffeurs, has the cash to get Jackson's family on, but Jackson and his family have to sneak on to be saved. Thanks to some help from our original hero, Adrian Helmsley, who told the president this was coming, world leaders open up the arks to take on more people. There are some scary moments as the world starts to flood, but the waters recede after about a month. Mankind, or at least some of it, gets a chance to start over. It has a solid story, good cast, and fairly impressive special effects, but it still didn't knock my socks off. It's a little uneven, and sometimes I found the pace distracting. But it's worth watching!

The Book of Eli (American, 2010)

Another decent, but not, in my opinion, great, post-apocalyptic film is *The Book of Eli*, released in 2010. Nevertheless, it did have a great cast, including Denzel Washington (Eli), Gary Oldman (Carnegie), Jennifer Beals (Claudia), Mila Kunis (Solara), and Michael Gambon (George). We start out 30 years after what appears to be a nuclear war, with Eli walking across the country headed west, surviving by scavenging and hunting. Eli occasionally comes across some of the usual lowlife thugs and road warriors you find in the apocalypse, but his fighting skills are more than enough to take out the trash.

Eli finds his way to a dumpy town that's located near a spring where he stops to get some water and recharge his iPod. As he waits for his iPod he takes out a gang of bad guys at the local bar. The leader of this less than vibrant community is a guy called Carnegie, who is kind of a ruthless gangster, but a book collector nevertheless. After watching Eli fight, Carnegie asks him to stay, and sends young Solara to convince him. Eli is a man of integrity and refuses her charms. It seems that Eli's mission is to protect a King James Bible, which seems to be rather scarce in the post-apocalyptic wasteland. Unlike other post-apocalyptic films, this one has a spiritual or religious dimension that's at the heart of Eli's wanderings.

Eli leaves to continue his westward mission, but Solara follows him, and the two end up being captured by Carnegie's men after a dramatic gunfight that includes a Gatling gun. Eli is wounded, and gives his Bible up to save Solara. After another battle, Carnegie heads back to town with his prize, and Eli and Solara head west. The Bible has a locking mechanism which, when opened, reveals to Carnegie's surprise that the Bible is written in Braille.

Eli and Solara make it west and arrive at a place of sanctuary, which oddly enough is Alcatraz. If you haven't already figured it out, at this point you see the spiritual aspect of Eli's mission, as he recites the entire Bible to the people there so it can be printed. What makes this all the more amazing is that Eli is actually blind, and he did all those amazing things along the way without sight. Eli succumbs to his wounds and dies, and Solara returns home. But copies of the Bible can now be printed and shared thanks to Eli's courage and resolve. It is well acted and enjoyable, but a bit tired, and maybe less engaging than others in this genre.

Cloverfield (American, 2008)

Some may argue that the 2008 film *Cloverfield* is not really a post-apocalyptic film since it's kind of New York–centric. Well, anytime you drop a nuclear bomb on NYC to take out a very large monster, that's apocalyptic enough for me. Besides, I lived in NYC! I was impressed with this one, and enjoyed it despite the film being a little jumpy due to the production method.

We start out with a romantic story of two young people, which is shot solely on a hand-held video camera. In fact, the entire movie is shot that way. Rob (Michael Stahl-David) and Beth (Odette Annable) are a lovely couple who are seen enjoying themselves in flashback videos. For reasons I don't recall, they break up, at least temporarily. Rob has accepted a new job in Japan, so his brother and friends throw a farewell party for him. Of course, Beth shows up with another guy, but then leaves in a huff after an argument with Rob. But now the plot thickens. While the party goes on, earthquakes or bomb denotations hit the city, which result in a black out. Now things go from bad to worse. As the partygoers leave the building, they almost get hit by the head of the Statue of Liberty. Chaos seems to reign as people are panicking, and you eventually see armed soldiers marching down the street.

In the distance, you can see and hear other explosions, and in the shadows you can see some kind of huge creature lurking between the buildings. Our group, and correctly so, decides to get out of Manhattan. The problem is that they choose to go to Brooklyn, and they soon find out that the Brooklyn Bridge is not a good place to be. The monster trashes the bridge, and Rob's brother, Jason (Mike Vogel), is among the casualties.

Despite this setback, Rob decides to save Beth, who is up around 59th Street. This is not an especially good idea, as, in addition to a really big monster, there are many little ones, too. But Rob convinces three friends to join him, and off they go. They manage to climb through damaged buildings and pull Beth from the rubble, and she appears to be saved.

The group manages to find its way to a safe zone in Midtown, and get on a couple of helicopters to get out of Dodge. Unfortunately, after a bomb is dropped on the creature, it gets pissed off and lunges at the helicopters, knocking them down in Central Park. The group gets mugged in the park—just kidding—but they do manage to keep that video recording going through all this mess. Rather impressive!

In the end, Rob and Beth are hiding in a tunnel waiting for the inevitable, frightened but in love, and you can hear air raid sirens in the background as, you guessed it, a nuke is dropped on Central Park. You can see flashback video of better days, but Rob and Beth are no more. This is an excellent film, and you could actually feel the fear and excitement as things developed. The creature lurking in the shadows among tall buildings in Midtown was really cool. The attempt by these kids to stay alive was very different than other films. This was an abrupt situation, and while most of their moves were initially based on panic, Rob's desire to save Beth was very purposeful. If you haven't already, see it.

The Invasion (American, 2007)

One film that came out in 2007 that might seem a little familiar is *The Invasion*. This film is essentially another remake of the 1956 film *Invasion of the Body Snatchers*. Now does that mean this is a bad film? Not necessarily, and how could any film with Nicole Kidman be bad? Ms. Kidman plays a psychiatrist in the film (Carol Bennell), and her leading man is Daniel Craig (Ben Driscoll).

The story starts out when the Space Shuttle Patriot crashes on its return to Earth. To make matters worse, some kind of space bacteria or spores are on the debris, and people become infected with a strange virus on contact. OK, now things start to get strange. Dr. Carol Bennell is treating a patient who tells her that her husband isn't really her husband. Yeah, he looks like him, acts like him, and knows all the facts, but it isn't him. Sound familiar? For those of you who were awake in the earlier chapters, you'll remember that 50 years ago in *Invasion of the Body Snatchers*, Dr. Miles Bennell (Kevin McCarthy) was treating people for similar claims. Family members were not really family members. Of course they weren't; they were freakin' aliens. By the way, you'll note that Nicole Kidman's character and Kevin McCarthy's character have the same name, Bennell. Must be related.

Like in the 1956 film, you can tell an alien by their emotionless kind of dopey demeanor. You know, all is well with the world. To get to that state, you have to have contact with alien bacteria, and then go to sleep. The transition to alien state is kind of disgusting; you look kind of slimy and you're in a cocoon. The aliens spend their time trying to infect others. Meanwhile, our hero, Dr. Bennell, is trying to stay awake and save her son, who seems to be immune to the virus. To protect herself and her son, she even shoots her boyfriend, Ben Driscoll, in the leg because he's become infected and she needs to get away from a bunch of aliens.

In one scene, Nicole Kidman's character is running around in the middle of the street trying to get help, reminiscent of Kevin McCarthy doing the same thing 50 years earlier. While it's doubtful I would stop for Kevin McCarthy, I'd be hard pressed not to stop for Nicole Kidman.

Carol gets her son, and is involved in some heavy-duty chase scenes where the infected try to take her out. In one scene, they are piled on top of a car she is driving, and she drives like a maniac to get them off. She and her son are rescued by a helicopter on top of a parking garage. Meanwhile, an inoculation is made that cures the infection. Everybody gets cured, and people go back to killing each other; a true victory for mankind. Not a bad flick, but I think it lacked the soul of the original.

The Happening (American, 2008)

Perhaps one of the more underrated post-apocalyptic films is *The Happening*. This film was released in 2008 with a cast that includes Mark Wahlberg, Zooey Deschanel, John Leguizamo, Betty Buckley, and Frank Collison. I really enjoyed this film—even though parts of the movie were really creepy—and I have seen it a few times.

The film starts off in Central Park in New York City where, for some inexplicable reason, people start killing themselves. One woman uses a knitting needle to get the job done; on a construction site, men walk off a roof, killing themselves instantly. In another scene, a policeman, after a casual conversation with a cab driver, pulls out his gun and blows his own brains out. This must have seemed like a good idea, because several other people pick up the gun and do the same thing.

Elliot Moore (Mark Wahlberg) is a science teacher in Philadelphia when news of these events starts to break. They close down the school and Elliot, his wife Alma (Zooey Deschanel), his friend Julian (John Leguizamo), and Julian's daughter Jess (Ashlyn Sanchez) decide to hop on a train and get out of Dodge. The bad news is that whatever it is that's spreading, much of the northeast seems to be affected. At first, folks think it's some kind of terrorism, but it soon becomes clear that something else is at work. As the saying goes, "Don't fool with Mother Nature." Maybe now she is fighting back.

After a short and somewhat chaotic train ride, the train stops and people are asked to leave it in some small town in Pennsylvania. It seems the train has lost all contact with the outside world. So the four are left stranded in the middle of nowhere. Time for Plan B. Julian makes the difficult decision to head for Princeton, where he believes his wife is. He leaves his daughter with Elliot and Alma, who end up with a plant nursery owner (Frank Collison). Despite his somewhat dopey demeanor, this man correctly believes the plants are responsible. He tells the others how plants can communicate, and do all sorts of things. Unlike in *The Day of the Triffids*, they don't seem to be able to move, but they do send out toxins that have a profound impact on people.

Sadly, Julian's choice to head for Princeton is a tragic mistake. After seeing remnants of mass suicides there, he also succumbs to the toxins in the air and takes his own life. Meanwhile, Elliot figures out that the more people that are together, the more likely the plants are to release the toxins. The three end up on an old farm inhabited by a rather creepy old lady who lets them stay the night. In the morning the toxins also infect the old woman, but Elliot, Alma, and Jess stay inside the house, in different locations so they're safer. Despite the risks of going outside, they decide they should be together. When they finally do go outside, nothing happens. The menace has passed—or so it seems. Flash forward three months, and Jess is now with her new adoptive parents. All is good—well, maybe not. In the next scene you are in Paris, France, and after a breeze that ruffles the leaves of plants and trees, you hear screaming in the background. The plants are at it again! It's a scary story, but wonderfully told.

20 Years After (American, 2008)

Another 2008 release was the film *20 Years After*. After watching it, I felt 20 years older. In fact, after watching this flick I have come to believe that if you have access to a junkyard and a few decent actors you can make a post-apocalyptic film. This one isn't a convincing story, although it could have been interesting if done differently. So how do you survive 20 years after a nuclear war? Yup, we are back to that again, and plagues, too. According to this flick, you chain smoke and listen to hillbilly music. That's a little bit of an exaggeration, but not that much.

As part of the mix, in this film you have a pregnant woman whom everybody seems to want, a black ventriloquist, a pirate radio DJ, and some rednecks hanging out in a cave. Not surprisingly, people have left the cities and spend their time scrounging for food, trying to avoid hostile rival groups, and occasionally trying to make contact with other survivors. One of the bad-guy survivors is a large, baldheaded, heavy dude who reminded me of Thor Johnson in *Plan 9 from Outer Space*. In any case, a key piece of the story is the trek of the pregnant young woman, Sarah (Azura Skye), who is trying to deliver her baby safely. This is the first child to be born in many years, and for that reason alone is very special.

Sarah starts out living in a basement with her mom, but leaves after hearing a radio broadcast, and comes to stay in a cave with other survivors. She wants out of there, and has to deal with a few wackos who want her baby, but she eventually leaves with DJ Michael (Joshua Leonard) and drives off into a post-apocalyptic sunset. This movie did little for me, but I can't fault the cast, who did a very credible job with what they had. Look, I do not claim to be a film expert; I can only tell you what I like, and this wasn't one of them. Probably because it didn't make me feel like it was real!

I Am Legend (American, 2007)

Perhaps one of the best virus movies, and for some, best zombie/virus movies, of the past twenty years was the 2007 release of *I Am Legend*. As far as I know, this is the third screen adaptation of Richard Matheson's novel of the same name. You may recall that the 1964 flick *The Last Man on Earth* and the 1971 film *Omega Man* were also adaptations of the same book. I actually think the 2007 movie is the best of the three, with *The Last Man on Earth* coming in a close second. It's the best because it's a great blend of a really good script, a great cast, and very effective special effects. I also found Will Smith's portrayal of main character Robert Neville excellent. At least through most of the film, his hopeful attitude of finding a cure was very effective. While it may tick off some, I did not include this film in the modern zombie section since I thought they were more like vampires, but who knows for sure?

You know, when they advertise drugs on TV that offer a cure for acne but have some nasty side effects like death or dementia, you may want to think twice about it. This is kind of what happens in this movie. Someone comes up with a cure for cancer, but the side effect includes the conversion of the human race to vampire-like creatures, leading to the downfall of civilization. Well, they probably should have used a larger test group.

Part of our story is told in flashbacks that show US Navy Virologist Robert Neville (Will Smith) trying to get his family out of New York City as the virus is spreading and chaos affects the city. The scenes where Neville is trying to evacuate his family are fairly intense, and serve as a good reminder that big cities are not the best place to be during the apocalypse. Sadly, Neville's wife and child are killed in a helicopter accident as they try to leave. Neville is left with only his German Shepard, Sam, to keep him company.

To fight off loneliness and to keep his sanity, Neville and his dog make daily rounds of the city looking for supplies and collecting information for his research. Most of the film seems to take place about three years later, and, as they roam around the city, you can see it's in great disrepair, and with wild animals also roaming the streets.

As he continues to search for a cure, which he experiments with on rats, he must return to his Washington Square apartment before dark every night to avoid being attacked by the infected. These creatures may be anemic looking, but they are very fast and strong, and impervious to pain. It appears that Neville discovers a treatment from his own blood, and decides to capture one of the infected to test it on. In the process, he captures the mate of the alpha male creature, which may not have been a good idea. These infected are not dummies; they actually set a trap for him, and he ends up losing his dog after they are attacked.

Neville has to kill his dog himself because she was infected, which understandably makes him a little wacko and sends him on a suicide mission to kill these creatures. He is nearly overrun, but is saved by two survivors who take him back to his place. Neville wakes up the next morning to find Anna (Alice Braga) and a little boy named Ethan (Charlie Tahan) eating breakfast. They believe that there is a survivor community in Vermont, and are planning to go there. Neville is unconvinced, and is more interested in curing the infected woman he has in his basement.

The good news is that he does find a cure, but the bad news is the infected don't seem to care. They attack his home and, in desperation, Neville gives Anna a vial of his own blood and hides her and the boy. As he makes a futile effort to reason with the alpha male, who keeps slamming himself into the protective glass wall, Neville blows himself and the creatures up with a grenade to stop them.

Anna and the boy escape and do find their way to a rather bucolic town in Vermont where they find other survivors, and Anna passes the cure on to the people there. Of the three film versions of Matheson's novel, this has the most positive ending. While in all three versions the lead character dies, in this production, a cure is found, which makes you believe there is some hope for the future. It definitely makes my post-apocalyptic hall of fame, and is one well worth watching. It's hard to believe the novel was written in 1954; it almost seems like it was written yesterday. That's my way of saying it's highly relevant!

Contagion (American, 2011)

Some people will argue that the film *Contagion*, released in 2011, is not really a post-apocalyptic film. After all, people do survive, and a cure is ultimately found. Well, this is one of those gray-area films. Keep in mind, you do get a pandemic, and social order does start to break down. Besides, I liked the movie, and it does show we are capable of getting beyond zombie-type viruses.

Our saga starts on a business trip to Hong Kong when Beth Emhoff (Gwyneth Paltrow) appears to catch the flu or something during dinner without knowing it. Beth has time for a quickie with an old boyfriend in Chicago before returning home to hubby Mitch Emhoff (Matt Damon) in Minneapolis. Her symptoms get really bad, and a couple of days later she is dead. To make matters worse, she managed to infect her son, Clark, and he dies, too. I found the autopsy sequence where they open up Gwyneth Paltrow's head to figure out what happened rather creepy.

After Beth's son dies, Mitch is held for observation, but he appears to be immune. His daughter from another marriage comes home to stay with him, but Mitch doesn't know if she is immune, too, and he tries to isolate her. Meanwhile, people all over the world start to succumb to the virus, and you can see social order start to break down as panic sets in. How can you have an apocalypse if there isn't widespread panic and looting?

Of course, our government isn't just standing around doing nothing. At the CDC, Dr. Ellis Cheever (Laurence Fishburne) dispatches one of his top people to figure out what the hell is going on. She traces the virus back to Beth, and another researcher at the CDC, Dr. Ally Hextall (Jennifer Ehie), figures out this disease is a combination of pig and bat viruses. I think they add a couple of names, which I can't pronounce or spell, so I'll use the easy one, Virus One, or MEV-1.

OK, so people are dropping like flies, and Dr. Cheever does a CDC no-no. He tells a family member to get out of Chicago, who, of course, tells others to do the same. Meanwhile, back at the CDC, our Dr. Hextall comes up with a possible vaccine. To expedite the testing process, she injects herself with it—and it works.

Hallelujah, we are saved! Well, maybe not, as it seems to take time to make the vaccine, so the CDC uses a lottery based on birth date to distribute the vaccine. Not good if you come up with the wrong number, which means you could be dead by the time your vaccine is delivered by FedEx. But that's the deal. Dr. Cheever, who was in trouble for telling his girlfriend to get out of Chicago, redeems himself by giving his vaccine to the son of a janitor in his building. Our original long-suffering hero, Mitch Emhoff, does manage to protect his daughter from the virus, but the process isn't easy—Mitch even goes so far as having his daughter celebrate her prom at his house to protect her, and yet give her a prom experience.

In the final scenes of the film, we find out that bat poop fell into a pig pen and was consumed by a pig, which was soon after prepared for dinner at a restaurant. The chef shook hands with Beth, and that's how it started. To put it bluntly, humanity was almost wiped out by bat poop. A final point: unlike most zombie flicks, films like *Contagion* are often more scary because they are far more believable. We only have to look back at our own history to prove that point.

Carriers (American, 2009)

As you can see, after we started the new millennium, diseases played a larger role in apocalypse films, and this was certainly evident in the 2009 film *Carriers*. However, unlike *Contagion*, we kind of start our movie in the aftermath of some unnamed outbreak that has destroyed most of the human race. Not a problem for our little crew, which includes Brain (Chris Pine), his girlfriend Bobby (Piper Perabo), his brother Danny (Lou Taylor Pucci), and his friend Kate (Emily VanCamp). They decide a road trip to the beach is the best way to deal with the apocalypse. In fairness to our group, they were just trying to rekindle memories from childhood as they headed to a beloved hotel on the beach.

We start out on the road—a side road of course, to avoid contact with the infected—as they head to their destination. They don't get too far before they run into Frank (Christopher Meloni) and his infected daughter, Jodie. Well, our group has rules, and not hanging out with the infected is at the top of the list. They try to escape, but in the end, they take Frank and Jodie with them in exchange for Frank's car. They seal little Jodie up in the back part of the car. They take Frank and Jodie to a place where a cure is being worked on, and revert back to rule number one when nothing is there. They leave the two and move on.

However, unknown to the rest of the group, Bobby tries to help Jodie and becomes infected. She doesn't say anything to the group, but at the next "close encounter of the bad kind" when they are captured by men at a hotel who tell them to disrobe, you can see that Bobby's infected. They get away from the armed men and seal Bobby off in the back of the car, but then leave her at a deserted gas station. Do we see a pattern forming here?

Since they are running low on gas, they manage to shoot two women in a car to get some. In the process, Brian gets shot in the leg, and the group stops at a house to find some medical supplies to treat him. Unfortunately, when Danny starts to treat him, they realize Brian is infected. Well, what do you do when your beloved brother is infected during the apocalypse? You shoot him—at his urging, of course—and move on.

In the final scene, Danny and Kate reach the beach they started out for, and you assume they live happily ever after—or at least the post-apocalyptic version of that. I would call this a "little" post-apocalyptic film, as there are few characters and not much in the way of special effects. It relies on a talented cast to tell the story, without a lot of bucks spent on the usual trappings of a post-apocalyptic film. Some may see this as a kind of rip off, but if you can capitalize on a popular theme, why not? If you look at many of these smaller apocalyptic films, this is fairly common.

Perhaps another issue that surfaces when you watch this movie is the utter ruthlessness of the effort to stay alive. Maybe this is just the imagination of an aging baby boomer, but films over the last 20 years or so seem to have become more violent in the survival process. In the early 1960s film *Panic in Year Zero,* the main character did rob a hardware store owner to help save his family, but he didn't shoot people for a couple of gallons of gas. One could probably make a good case that survive at all costs is the reality, and it seems that today's audiences have come to expect this type of reaction.

Plague (Australian, 2015)

For whatever reason, Australian filmmakers have made post- apocalyptic films something of a cottage industry. Some have made a significant splash with movie goers; others have not. Some, despite low budgets, like *These Final Hours*, have sent a powerful message. This is probably not true for the 2015 Australian film *Plague*, but it still was a competent film. Continuing on our virus run, this flick is about the impact of a virus, which seems to have wiped out most of the human race in Australia. And of course, if that weren't bad enough, infected people often turn into cannibalistic monsters.

We start our little adventure when a band of five people are holed up at a farm trying to find some shelter. Our hero—and that's something of an exaggeration—Evie (Tegan Crowley) is hoping her husband John (Scott Marcus) will find them, and she doesn't want to leave until he gets there. Some of the group feel the farm is no longer safe and want to leave. As far as this group of five knows, they are the last people on Earth, but they manage to reduce the human population by 20% when one guy shoots another over the leave or stay debate. Rather amazing!

The other three go. Evie stays, and hubby John shows up soon after. John is a college professor in the social science area, so his survival skills are rather limited. I should add that John initially comes off as a wimp. When the farmhouse is almost overrun by cannibalistic creatures, he decides to blow his brains out instead of protecting his wife. However, Charlie (Steven Kennedy) comes by and saves them, and offers to protect them. He even gives them supplies. What a nice guy; human decency is not gone!

Not so fast—it seems Charlie's real interest is Evie. Well, for all he knows, she is the last woman on Earth. Charlie may not be a nice guy, but he knows how to survive, and when John has an asthma attack, Evie makes Charlie go out and find some medicine for him. Charlie, being a resourceful guy (and kind of a creep in my estimation) returns with the medicine, and John is saved. The price for this "human kindness" is that Evie is basically forced to have sex with Charlie.

John seems to believe that they need Charlie to survive, and even allows Charlie to drag Evie off into a barn to rape her, but when a soldier comes by, John figures there may be a safe place to go, so he somehow overpowers the soldier and then shoots Charlie. Unfortunately, before he dies, Charlie shoots Evie in the arm.

John gets Evie into a car and they drive off, but what kind of post-apocalyptic film would let them drive off into the sunset? The car breaks down, and Evie seems spent, but John urges her to go on. Has John finally manned up and tried to face his responsibilities? Maybe not, because when he realizes she might not be able to make it, he plans to leave her behind. Too bad for him that Evie figures that out and shoots him in the leg to give her time to get away from the cannibalistic creatures (zombies) that end up devouring John. Nice to have a happy apocalypse ending as Evie continues to walk down the road.

This is another one of those low budget little post-apocalyptic films. It's well acted to be sure, but not particularly compelling. Unlike some of the other films in this genre, there is very little hope in this film. It presents a very cynical view of human nature, and you wonder if we are worth saving after watching it. Earlier films may present horrible circumstances, but this is truly a dark message. Self-interest is above all things, and survival is all that counts. Like in the film *Carriers*, where people did some rather horrible things to survive, including killing loved ones and strangers for a couple of gallons of gas, John's willingness to abandon his wife sends a rather chilling message. Perhaps there are no friends in the apocalypse!

Refuge (American, 2013)

But who says there are no good guys in the apocalypse? In the 2013 film *Refuge*, humanity may have lost its way, but not totally. The world is plagued by some sort of bacterial outbreak that, despite efforts to contain it, ends up destroying most of humanity. Sound familiar? In this grim and rather sobering film, people tend to hole up on their own and avoid contact with others, as is the case with Jack (Carter Roy) and his wife and child, who, along with someone they helped along the way, try to stay hidden in a house in the woods. Jack's job is to forage for food and try to take care of his family. And make sure his family stays out of sight.

After picking up injured stranger Russell (Sebastian Beacon) who was on the outs with a group of marauding bad guys, Jack and crew are under siege by those marauding bad guys, but fight their way out. Their friend ends up injured, and eventually dies. Russell convinces them to join up with his brother, but they end up getting lost in the woods, and are confronted with some very bad guys. While Jack is off trying to figure out where they are, his wife and daughter are taken by a group of predators who want to enslave them, and Russell manages to get killed in the process. Did you ever notice that the bad guys in these movies always have bad teeth? Didn't people practice good dental hygiene before the apocalypse?

When Jack finds his wife and daughter in the company of two very dangerous men, he threatens to shoot them if they don't let his family go. They offer to give him his wife, but want to keep the daughter. Before he can take them out, their buddies ambush Jack and shoot him with a crossbow. Just when things look the worst, another group attacks the bad guys and saves the family. In the scheme of things, this is a good thing in the apocalypse—you know, good over evil! The film travels a very familiar road—maybe too familiar—but it seems more realistic than many, and the cast is good. You can give the gritty effects, realism, and good acting decent marks, but the story offers nothing really new. It's hardly a must see, but I still enjoyed the film.

Parts Per Billion (American, 2014)

When it comes to diseases that can wipe out mankind, Mother Nature isn't the only one we have to worry about. Yes, nukes weren't bad enough, so we had to invent biological weapons just to make sure we can kill everybody. That's the kind of story line in the 2014 film *Parts Per Billion*. In this movie, some kook in the Middle East decides to use a biological weapon to take out the other side. So what else is new! If you're wondering what the title means, it refers to the level of pathogens in the air. At a certain level, the pathogens become fatal. If you want a better explanation, ask a science major.

Despite a strong cast that includes Frank Langella and Gena Rowlands, this film didn't click for me. While the storyline is how the dispersion of pathogens released from biological weapons in the Middle East basically destroys the human race, the actual story focuses on the lives of three couples. At the start of the film, you see the expected panic and breakdown of social order as the pathogens take their toll. The plot is certainly interesting enough, and the first part of the movie gets your attention. However, the back and forth with flashbacks, which really want you to understand the emotional ties between three couples facing the apocalypse, is a bit hard to follow.

While you get the picture that these couples are in love with each other, the apocalypse theme gets lost in the shuffle. Probably because of the flashbacks and the couples fixation, you don't get a really good sense of how bad things are out there. Sometimes when we go to the current time you can see bodies lying in the streets, but it doesn't really register. In one scene, where Frank Langella's character is wheeling Gena Rowlands's character around town in her wheelchair, you see dead people on the streets, but they almost seem like props to remind you that you're watching an apocalypse movie. In one of the few more realistic scenes, a close friend of one of the couples is shot in a convenience store when he can't pay for the items he needs.

The film didn't seem well organized, and it was hard to follow at times. This was no fault of the actors—they were convincing—but their roles were not always in synch with the main theme. OK, so I'm an apocalypse movie nut, and may not appreciate "apocalypse subtlety."

Into the Forest (Canadian, 2015)

Well, we have had to cope with nukes, viruses, and meteors, but what about blackouts? Come on, many will say that, compared to the other worries, can this really be a legitimate post-apocalyptic theme? All I can say is, yes, it can. As you will see later in the chapter on TV apocalypse, blackouts, or power loses, can be very deadly. In some survival shows they point out that without power, 90% of the population would be dead in a year. With that sobering thought, we can move on to a little movie released in 2015 called *Into the Forest*. This is kind of a low budget, narrowly focused, no special effects type flick. It isn't going to make it on anybody's top-ten list, but I thought it was an engaging film that at times was very realistic. This is due in no small part to two talented young actresses, Ellen Page, who plays Nell, and Evan Rachel Wood, who plays Eva. This is basically the cast, and somehow they make it work.

The film starts out with these two young women living with their dad in a cozy forest home a few miles outside of a small town. For reasons never quite explained the power goes out, and the story goes from one about a mild annoyance to a fight for survival. Eva is upset that she can't play music to practice for a dance test she is about to take. That will be the least of her problems as time goes on.

One of the interesting things about this film is that not only do you not know what caused the blackout, you also don't know how widespread it is. When Nell's boyfriend stops by, he decides to go with a group to Boston, where he hears they have power. Since I think this town is probably out west, that is quite a hike. My guess—and yes, it's because I watch all these movies—is that the blackout is widespread, and mankind is on the brink of extinction.

In any event, early on the girls and their dad are doing OK, despite the hardship imposed by the loss of power. But then Dad manages to kill himself in a chainsaw accident, and the girls are now on their own. They prove to have very good survival skills, but when Eva gets raped by one of the townies, the girls' struggle becomes far more challenging. Eva ends up pregnant from the attack, but wants to keep the baby. Not surprisingly, food becomes more scarce, and the girls have to extend themselves. At one point, Nell decides to hunt wild boar, but nobody told her about recoil, so when she shoots a boar from a perch in a tree the blast knocks her out of the tree. She does get the boar though!

Eventually, Eva gives birth to a baby boy, but the house they live in is literally falling down around them. Eva decides they should burn the house down and move on. Nell agrees, and they set fire to the house—

not an easy thing to do when it's pouring rain, but they do it. With a few belongings they head off into the forest, probably to live in a little hollowed-out tree Nell used to go to. This is an interesting flick that I think works because it focuses on how the girls survive, despite being a low budget type film.

The Hunger Games (American, 2012)

Perhaps one of the biggest budget post-apocalyptic films of the new millennium is *The Hunger Games*, released in 2012. It's hard not to like this one, which takes place in a rather depressing future that brings back gladiatorial combat for the amusement of the masses and as some kind of punishment for a prior rebellion. The nation of Panem is broken into 12 districts, and the deal is that once a year two tributes, one boy and one girl, are selected from each district to fight in the Hunger Games. Yes, the fight is to the death, but you do get to eat great food and stay in a nice place for a few days before you're killed in the games. And you do get to live if everybody else is killed.

In District 12, the lucky winners are Katniss Everdeen (Jennifer Lawrence) and Peeta Mellark (Josh Hutcherson). Katniss becomes something of a sensation when she volunteers to take her younger sister's place. Katniss and Peeta are escorted to the capital city for the games, and have one Haymitch Abernathy (Woody Harrelson), a former District 12 winner, assigned to them as a mentor. Haymitch won the games in his time, but he is a drunk now, and not particularly helpful at first. But how could anyone not like Woody Harrelson, who played a zombie-hating redneck in *Zombieland* (2009)? Based on his initial style, it doesn't look like his mood changed much from that movie to this one.

Haymitch does come around, and he tries to give them guidance, including the importance of getting sponsors, who can help give you an edge during the contest. This is good advice, especially for Katniss who, despite her beauty, is not the most sociable person around. But her charms do capture Peeta's attention, and during a TV promotion for the games he tells the world he is in love with Katniss. Young love is wonderful, but, in this case, you may have to kill your lover in the games, which could be a real bummer.

The games go off, and somehow Katniss manages to survive, and so does Peeta, although he does get injured. While initially game rules were revised to allow two from the same district to survive, the game organizer changes his mind, and says one has to go. Katniss refuses to accept this ruling, and she and Peeta decide to eat poisonous berries in protest. The government recants at the last moment, and they are saved. Unfortunately, this cannot be said about the game organizer, who does get to eat the berries. This film was excellent, and had a great cast including Stanley Tucci as the Hunger Games show host, and Donald Sutherland as the evil President Snow. The next couple of installments of this series were good, but could not match the charm of the first film.

The Road (American, 2009)

If you find yourself in very good spirits and are looking for a way to come down, try watching *The Road*. If you are not depressed after watching this film, see a doctor. Released in 2009, this film is based on the book of the same title by Cormac McCarthy. After reading a *New York Times* book review on the novel, I decided to read it. As is often the case, the book was better than the film. But I was excited when the film was produced, because I liked the book so much.

The film starts after some extinction-level event that turns the world into a desolate wasteland that's almost completely devoid of life. You never know what caused it, but the effects are horrific. For the most part, you see a very gray landscape that offers little hope. I think this post-apocalyptic film almost corners the market in hopelessness. The only people who are around are scavengers or worse. The main characters are a man (Viggo Mortenson) and his young son (Kodi Smith-McPhee). The man's wife (Charlize Theron) is featured in flashbacks, but for reasons that aren't totally clear, she heads off into the woods by herself earlier in the apocalypse.

The basic storyline is the man and boy heading off on "the road," looking for supplies and heading for the coast where they hope things will be better. This is not an easy task when you have to avoid cannibalistic hordes and other crazies. By the way, supplies are rather limited, and the man and boy are basically starving. One of the high points in their journey is when they find an old can of Coke, which the man gives to the boy, who is amazed by the taste. A less positive experience is when they are almost caught by a band of cannibals, and the man has to use one of his last two bullets to take out one of them.

Things aren't all bad—mostly, but not all bad—because they do manage to stumble on a bunker filled with food. They stuff themselves for a couple of days, but get spooked by some noises near the bunker and move on. They do take some supplies with them. In one of the few acts of humanity in this movie, they stumble on an old man (Robert Duvall) on the road, and share some food with him. Unfortunately, while the man (Viggo Mortensen's character) is taking a swim, another person steals their food. They catch up to him, take the food back, and steal his clothes. The boy is upset about treating the thief that way, so they leave his clothes and some food behind for him.

After wandering into a trashed town, the man gets shot in the leg with an arrow, but takes out the wacko with a flare gun. Now, most father-son activities center on playing catch, or throwing around a football—not so much in this flick. Instead, the man tries to teach his son how to blow his own brains out with their one remaining bullet. Weakened by the arrow, and sickness, the man eventually dies, leaving the little boy alone. However, even this movie has bright spots; the boy is befriended by a man and his wife and family who take him in. So, I guess you can say the father completed his mission by protecting his son, but for how long?

The Day (American, 2011)

Another rather bleak and depressing film that falls into the "little movie" category is *The Day*, which was released in 2011. Now this film is never going to make anybody's top-ten list, but it is a solid film that is well acted and tells a decent story.

This is one of those movies that starts out in a post-apocalyptic landscape, but you are never sure how we got there. All I know is that there are five survivors banded together looking for food and safety. In addition to very limited resources, they are also confronted with gangs of cannibals who are damned pissed they can no longer go to the Out-back Steakhouse. This cannibalistic theme is more prominent in recent post-apocalyptic films than in earlier decades. Up until more recent films, we seemed to focus more on zombies eating people, rather than people eating people. It makes a lot of sense, though, since finding food at the local Trader Joe's or Wal-Mart isn't a real option in an apocalypse. This also suggests that filmmakers want to jazz up the post-apocalyptic theme, and try to scare us even more!

However, our little band of five actually includes an ex-cannibal, and it soon becomes a band of four after one of them is killed in a booby trap at an abandoned farmhouse where they sought shelter. While the farmhouse has plenty of food supplies, this stuff belongs to a local band of cannibals. Time to leave! But before they can, a small band of the cannibals finds them and threatens to come back, to eat them, of course. Our group will have none of this, and kills them all.

The problem is, they know they can't run. One member of the group is sick, and they have only limited ammo. To make matters worse, they discover that one of the group, Mary (Ashley Bell), is a former cannibal, which they didn't know until now. They beat and torture her, believing she is probably in on their current woes. However, she convinces them she's not, that she is tormented by guilt about her previous life, and will fight to the end to stop the cannibal band. She proves true to her word, fighting fiercely through the night, but is betrayed by one of the group and is left for dead. However, Adam (Shawn Ashmore), who tortured Mary a few hours earlier, goes back to help her. He saves her, and they take out the cannibal band, but he dies from wounds suffered in the battle. In a nice finishing touch to the movie, the cannibal leader's daughter, who killed one of our band of four, receives justice from Mary, who slits the girl's throat after she approaches Mary. Then our heroine, Mary, walks off into the post-apocalyptic landscape by herself. Again, this movie is not a top-of-the-list flick, but it is well done and worth watching.

To Survive (American, 2014)

On the not-so-hot side is the 2014 film *To Survive.* The good news is that I survived watching it, and for a while I did have my doubts. This is one of those "let's try to capitalize on the post-apocalyptic film craze, but let's not put too much into it" movies. I can't blame the actors, who did a credible job, but they didn't have much to work with.

We start off in a post-apocalyptic world, but I'm not sure what caused it. A survivor is walking through the woods when he hears cries from a woman who has been attacked by a marauding band of bad guys. Remember when you were a kid and your mother told you not to talk to strangers? Well, this rule is especially true in the apocalypse! The woman dies and the man heads for a town where he hooks up with another man, his daughter, and his father. The murderous band kills the man's father, but our group of three decides to head south, to try to avoid the bad guys.

On the road, they manage to save a couple of people from the creeps, but after a supply run, two of their members get killed fighting off the bad guys. This includes the little girl's father, and now, having lost everyone, she is all alone. Not so fast! Our original hero, who was very much a loner in the beginning of the film, promised the girl's father he would take care of her if anything ever happened to him, and he does. The film ends when our hero, a woman he saved, and the little girl drive off into the sunset. This is hardly an epic film, but I saw it on Amazon, so I don't feel too bad about it.

These Final Hours (Australian, 2013)

A very effective little movie that came out in 2013 was the Australian film *These Final Hours.* Unlike many post-apocalyptic films, this one offered no hope. There weren't any NASA spaceships that would blow the asteroid out of the sky, or bunkers to save some; this is a *fait accompli.*

The film starts out after a meteor has struck the North Atlantic, and western Australia has 12 hours left.

The film centers on James (Nathan Phillips) and his girlfriend, Zoe (Jessica De Grow). James starts out as kind of a jerk, leaving his girlfriend behind at the end of the world. He decides that partying is a better idea, and tries to connect with some buddies at an end-of-the-world party. Even though the focus of this film is mostly on James, you can see civilization crumble in Earth's final hours. When he gets to the party, people are having wild sex, doing drugs, and even playing Russian roulette.

However, on route to the party, James has his car stolen, and ends up rescuing a ten-year-old little girl, Rose, who is being attacked by two perverts. After killing them, he tries to dump the little girl on his sister, but his sister is already dead. Time for Plan B, which is to head for the party. At the party, James seems to be lost, and not much into what's going on. He then decides to try his mother's place, and then goes on to the little girl's aunt's house. Upon arrival, they eventually find everyone dead, including the little girl's father. After Rose insists on seeing her father, James tells Rose about Zoe, and Rose tells him to patch things up. James makes an all-out effort to see Zoe, and even after his car breaks down he runs the rest of the way and finds her on the beach.

At first, she is angry with him for leaving her, but soon the couple are in an embrace, facing the inevitable firestorm that kills them both. In some ways, the ending is similar to *Deep Impact*, but substitute tidal wave for firestorm, and daughter and father for James and Zoe. In many ways, this was a really powerful film. Nathan Phillips does an outstanding job playing a character who starts out as a very shallow person, but comes to terms with human decency when it almost doesn't matter. Grim and realistic, this is worth watching.

Cell (American, 2016)

Of more recent vintage is Stephen King's 2016 film *Cell*. Perhaps a better title would have been *Cell Phone Apocalypse*. I want to say up front that

I read and really enjoyed King's book, but the film was something of a disappointment. The film had a really good cast, but the movie script didn't translate into a good movie. Maybe there was too much ground to cover in a two-hour movie. If nothing else, the film gave us something else to worry about; in addition to nuclear war, meteors, viruses, and aliens, we now have to watch out for cell phones, too. Go figure!

Clayton Riddell (John Cusack), an artist from Maine, is in Boston to nail down a book illustration contract. For reasons I'm not totally sure about, an electronic pulse is sent out worldwide over cell phones. You know when they tell you bad things can happen when you text? This is way worse. The pulse turns everybody who happens to be on their phones at the time into rabid killers. These people are affectionately referred to as "phoners" in the book and movie. In the beginning of the film, you can see all kinds of chaos erupting in Boston as people become raving maniacs. You can see planes falling from the sky, fires, and people attacking one another.

Our hero, Clayton, is no dummy, so after connecting with Tom McCourt (Samuel L. Jackson) and Alice Maxwell (Isabelle Fuhrman), he decides to head back to Maine to try to connect with his estranged wife and son. This sounds like a plan, but the group must contend with hordes of phoners along the way. After stopping at Tom's house, they head north and link up with school headmaster Charles Ardai (Stacy Keach) and one of his students. Together they take out a large horde of phoners who are recharging, just like your cell phone, in a football field during the night. They do this by running over them, dousing them with gasoline, and setting them on fire.

After some additional adventures, which include getting attacked by phoners in a bar, hanging with some redneck anti-phoners, and killing Clay's wife who is also a phoner, Clay continues to look for his son while the others head north. Clay eventually reconnects with his son, Johnny, but it's downhill from there. Johnny is a phoner, too, but not a complete one. The notion that Johnny can be fixed by another signal is presented, but it's not totally clear about what happens to him. The ending is confusing; at one point you see Clay walking with his son down a lonely road, in another sequence, Clay is seen in a horde of phoners. The film has its moments, but this is certainly not a must-see flick.

Goodbye World (American, 2013)

Another one of those films that shouldn't be on your "bucket list" is *Goodbye World,* released in 2013. A better name might have been *Friends* [the TV show] *Meets the Apocalypse.* Basically, the film shows how a bunch of dysfunctional 30 somethings try to hide out at the end of the world. We are led to believe that James and Lilly Palmer (Adrian Grenier, Kerry Bishe) and their daughter have gone off the grid to supposedly avoid a societal meltdown. The film is set someplace in the wilderness, but for all I know it was filmed in Ozone Park in Queens.

As far as I can figure, it appears that the apocalypse was caused by a virus-infected text message that took out the power grid. No more texts for me! Soon, old boyfriends and girlfriends arrive at the Palmer's home in the wilderness. It looks fairly good, since the Palmers are well stocked and prepared for just about everything. Of course, who would have figured that an old boyfriend would start hitting on James's wife, and that a young student, who was sleeping with another member of our dysfunctional "breakfast club," would go a bit wacko and leave the group. She also tells a rogue group of National Guard members about all the cool stuff the Palmer group has.

It's no surprise that the guard members and some local rednecks decide to take the Palmers' stuff. But after taking some abuse and bullying from a guardsman, a member of the group shoots the bad guardsman, and James decides to share his stuff with the others. Two of the group ride off into the sunset to help others, while the rest of the group decides to have a go at living off the land. In post-apocalyptic films, this is as close as you get to a happy ending. I can't fault the cast for a weak film; it was a dopey script that often felt like a soap opera.

10 Cloverfield Land (American, 2016)

OK, you're driving down the road and you get rear-ended by some nut job, and the next thing you know you're chained to a wall in a concrete bunker, and some fat guy tells you it's the end of the world. Sounds implausible? Well then, you need to see *10 Cloverfield Lane*, a film released in 2016. Now, I left out that our heroine, Michelle (Mary Elizabeth Winstead), was listening to some scary reports on the radio about major blackouts when this rear-end collision happened.

The proprietor of this homey bunker is a guy named Howard (John Goodman), who is a rather scary and intense dude, and he fills Michelle in on what has happened, and reminds her that he saved her by bringing her to his shelter. Eventually, she gets the grand tour, and meets her other shelter buddy, Emmett (John Gallagher Jr.). This is one of those small-cast apocalyptic films that works because of the talent of the cast, especially John Goodman, who is great in everything he does.

Over dinner, Michelle manages to drug Howard and steal his key to the exit tunnel, because, as she remembers the details of her accident, she realizes it was Howard's truck that drove her off the road. Hurray, the world is not destroyed after all. Well, maybe not, because as Michelle attempts to leave, she sees one of Howard's neighbors all burned up and trying to get in. Sounds like it's time for a new strategy, since it appears the apocalypse really did happen. So the three decide to "just get along" and enjoy bunker life. But when an air ventilator fails, Michelle is elected to fix it. In the process, she discovers a second escape hatch with the word "help" scratched on it.

Michelle shares her findings with Emmett, and the plot gets a little confusing at this point—at least for me it does. It appears that Howard may have killed a local woman, and our duo plan to exit, apocalypse or no apocalypse. Unfortunately for Emmett, Howard finds out about this plan and shoots and kills him. Michelle flees when she finds Emmett's body in a vat of acid. Horrified, she kicks the vat over, burning Howard and starting a fire. She puts on the HAZMAT suit she made and leaves the bunker. Out in the world, she sees creepy alien types, and now it's clear it was aliens, not the Russians, who caused the apocalypse. The radio tells of survivor camps, and as she drives off into the sunset, she knocks down a mailbox with the address 10 Cloverfield Lane. This is a very entertaining film, well scripted and well acted.

The Survivalist (British, 2015)

A 2015 film that I saw recently on Amazon Prime was *The Survivalist,* which is another of those "little" apocalyptic movies. This is hardly a great movie, but certainly a solid effort. What it lacked in scope and special effects, it more than made up for with a gritty and rather dark realism. As far as I can figure, it seems that oil production declines significantly—not sure why—and the human population follows suit, which seems to result in economic collapse.

As the film opens, we find the survivalist (Martin McCann) tending his garden in the woods. He seems to be the strong silent type, since he has been alone in the woods for seven years, and he isn't even talking to himself. Soon he is approached by an older woman, Kathryn (Olwen Fouere), and her young daughter Milja (Mia Goth), who ask for food and shelter for the night. In return, they grant him the sexual favors of Milja. This is essentially the cast, except for some bad guys who surface now and then.

Reluctantly, the man overcomes his suspicions concerning the two women, and they forge a survivalist-type relationship. They forage and try to plant food, but it's a meager existence, and they are on the verge of starving. Things are so bad that Kathryn and Milja consider bumping off the survivalist to have more food. Plans change when some wacko in the forest captures Milja, and while the survivalist manages to free her and kill the bad guy, he gets wounded in the process. The women help treat the wounded man, and eventually he gets better, only to find they are now under siege by six raiders.

The raiders trash the little farm. Milja tries to give herself an abortion, and Kathryn is still into getting rid of the survivalist. However, Milja decides to poison Kathryn and "stand by her man." Kathryn dies, with a little help from the survivalist, and the raiders return. This time, a serious battle ensues, and while the survivalist kills one, he is seriously wounded, but uses his harmonica to draw attention to him and allow time for Milja to escape. The bad guys get the survivalist, but Milja manages to escape. A few days later, she stumbles on a compound of people who have set up a large survivor camp. However, to be let in, the group must approve her. While she is waiting, a guard asks if she is pregnant, and Milja says yes. The film ends!

The narrow focus of the film made it slow moving at times, but it certainly seemed realistic. While it was not as dark a film as *The Road,* it was still rather depressing. Perhaps this is what the face of the apocalypse really looks like. No zombies or aliens to trash, just people trying to survive!

Chapter Eight: Modern Zombie Films

28 Days Later (British, 2002)

In 2002, a great British zombie film was released called *28 Days Later*. This film had a really interesting script, and while I didn't know many of the actors, they were wonderful. The film was fortunate enough to include one of my favorite current actors, Brendan Gleeson, who has played everything from a dopey sheriff in Maine to Winston Churchill.

The story starts out with a bunch of animal activists breaking into a lab to free some chimps. Bad idea! These chimps are infected with some kind of rage virus that is very contagious. So one of our animal liberators gets infected, and she, in turn, infects everyone else.

OK, fast-forward 28 days, and we find Jim (Cillian Murphy) awake in a deserted hospital after being in a coma as a result of a bicycle accident. After leaving the hospital, Jim quickly learns that something really bad happened, as the streets of London are deserted, too. Jim finds his way to a church and gets attacked by an infected priest. Fleeing the priest, he ends up attracting more of these zombie types. To make matters worse, these are fast zombies that can run and chase you down, not the usual types you see ambling along in typical zombie movies. Now, I'm using the term zombies, because what else are you going to call creatures that try to bite you and attack you on sight? In any case, Jim is saved from the infected chasing him by Selena (Naomie Harris) and Mark (Noah Huntley), who fill him in on the collapse of their world thanks to the spread of the viral infection.

Jim wants to find his parents, so the three trek to his house. They find the parents dead, and Mark is attacked and appears to be infected. Selena kills him in an instant. Apparently, the zombie conversion process is extremely fast. Selena uses this opportunity to warn Jim that she would also kill him in a heartbeat if he gets bitten. There's something to be said for knowing where you stand in any relationship, even if it's during the apocalypse.

As they look for a safe haven, Jim and Selena see Christmas lights blinking in an apartment building. After a rather scary entrance to the building, they meet Frank (Brendan Gleeson) and his daughter Hannah (Megan Burns)—finally, two other survivors. With supplies dwindling, the group heads off to find what they believe is a safe haven in Manchester. Unfortunately, when a drop of blood falls in Frank's eye he becomes infected, but is taken out by a group of soldier survivors, who take the other three to a mansion fortress.

Are things getting better? Not so much. These soldiers are a little out there, to say the least, and their commander (Christopher Eccleston) has promised them women. The soldiers try to attack Selena and Hannah, but a confused battle that includes infected and soldiers takes place, and Selena and Hannah escape with some help from Jim, but Jim is shot in the process. However, 28 days later, Jim is recovering in a country home, and together they've made a large quilt that says "hello" on it that they place in a field outside. A jet plane flies over them and Selena asks Jim, "Do you think they saw us this time?" This is an excellent film that spawned a sequel, *28 Weeks Later.*

28 Weeks Later (British, 2007)

My approach to "end of days" flicks is to avoid going into sequels in any depth. As far as 28 Weeks Later is concerned (2007), it was a well done movie with a similar plot, but with a few added twists. The film starts out 28 weeks after the virus hit London, and the American military has stepped in to restore order. Actually, this film was made about five years after the original. Well, you know order can't be maintained, or you don't have much of a film. So of course, there is another outbreak, and as the military tries to restore order, two kids who are believed to be survivors try to avoid everybody, but get help from a few soldiers. They were supposed to be left behind in Wembley Stadium to ensure containment, but a helicopter pilot takes them to France. Of course, 28 days later, a request for help comes from France. In a final scene, you can see infected headed to the Eiffel Tower.

Dawn of the Dead (American, 2004)

OK, so I'm not big on sequels and remakes, but as I mentioned earlier, one of my favorite zombie flicks is the 2004 version of Dawn of the Dead. This is a remake of the 1978 George Romero classic. So why did I like this better? Well, character development was better, and I enjoyed the interaction between the survivors, even though many would be picked off by the end of the film. Also, the cast was really strong: Sarah Polley, Ving Rhames (a classic zombie hunter), Michael Kelly, Ty Burrell, Mekhi Phifer, Jake Weber, and Boyd Banks, a guy who often shows up in Romero zombie movies.

While the plots of the two Dawn of the Dead films are similar in that the characters spend time hiding out in shopping malls, the second film doesn't have to deal with biker gangs and overly aggressive SWAT teams, just a lot of zombies and some inconsiderate survivors.

We start our little zombie adventure when Ana (Sarah Polley) is finishing a long nursing shift at a local hospital. It isn't totally clear how the zombie apocalypse starts, but Ana is talking to another nurse about complications involved with a patient who got bit in a bar fight. In any case, Ana goes home and spends some quality time with her husband, but misses some emergency announcements about the spread of a zombie virus. Meanwhile, a neighbor's daughter becomes infected and attacks Ana's husband, turning him into a flesh-eating zombie. I should point out these are the fast zombies, so you'd better be quick. They don't amble along; they sprint.

Ana gets away from her husband, and when she gets outside, her neighbors are running amok. The zombies are chasing the non-zombies, and one guy who threatens to shoot Ana if she comes near him gets run down by an ambulance. Scary stuff! Ana gets away in her car, but is almost forced out by a panicked man, and ends up crashing into a tree. When she comes to, she is almost shot by Officer Ken Hall (Ving Rhames), but after walking a short way, they meet some other survivors, and they all head for a nearby shopping mall for protection.

After a couple of minor zombie encounters at the mall, one of which results in a pregnant woman in their party being bitten, they head to the top floor where security is located. Unfortunately, the security crew, headed by a guy named CJ (Michael Kelly), is a little out there, and not all that excited about hosting some new visitors. After some nasty encounters between the groups, folks settle in, and are joined by a few more people.

After disposing of a couple of infected people, and with supplies dwindling, the group decides to leave the mall, take a boat owned by Steve (Ty Burrell)—one of their group and probably the biggest jerk in the apocalypse—and head for an island. To do this, they reinforce two shuttle buses and drive through the zombie-infested city. The trip is almost a disaster, with one bus crashing and the other eventually overrun by zombies. Most of their crew is killed, including Steve the jerk, but CJ, who was kind of a creep in the beginning, actually sacrifices himself for the group by blowing up a bunch of zombies in the second shuttle bus. Four survivors head out to sea to find a "zombie-free" island. Unfortunately, when they land on an island, they are chased by another bunch of zombies. So much for happy endings, but this is a top-notch zombie and post-apocalyptic film. In fact, I would rank this in the top three of "pure zombie" movies, along with the original *Night of the Living Dead* and *World War Z.*

Land of the Dead (Canadian, 2005)

I find the next zombie film of this period, *Land of the Dead* (2005), somewhat less impressive, despite being directed by George Romero and featuring an excellent cast including Simon Baker, John Leguizamo, Dennis Hopper, and Robert Joy. The cast also included Boyd Banks, who is a nice guy I met at some of the sci-fi conventions, as a zombie butcher.

In this flick, the zombie apocalypse is basically over, and the best you can do is try to stay away from them. People do this by living in walled cities. One of these walled cities is in Pittsburg, a hell of a place to avoid zombies, which is protected by rivers and an electric fence. Of course, even in the zombie apocalypse you have to have class struggle. So the rich people live in luxury condos in a beautiful high-rise building, while the rest of the folks hang out in the junkyard estates. So much for equality! Dennis Hopper plays the ruthless leader of this place, but he isn't all bad, since he came up with Dead Reckoning, which is a fancy armored vehicle that is used for zombie culling and other nasty things.

Dead Reckoning is commanded by the highly respected Riley Denbo (Simon Baker), who decides to pack it in after a recent zombie excursion. The evil Kaufman (Dennis Hopper), who runs the show, is a nasty guy and won't even help those who are loyal to him. One of his henchmen, Cholo DeMora (John Leguizamo), is looking for a condo in Kaufman's neighborhood, but Kaufman doesn't want any trailer trash in his building. That doesn't sit well with Cholo, who takes over Dead Reckoning to get even and threatens to take out Kaufman's buildings.

Now, if things were not getting bad enough, it seems the zombies are starting to show learning abilities. Just what you need, zombies with high IQs! Well, Riley comes out of a rather short retirement and manages to get Dead Reckoning back from Cholo. Riley tries to convince Cholo to come with him, but Cholo decides to head back and visit Kaufman. Unfortunately, he gets bitten and turns into a zombie. Nevertheless, he still goes after Kaufman.

Meanwhile the zombies are massing, and it seems they can now walk under water, which they do, and they launch an attack against the city. They start killing humans, who appear to be trapped by the fence that was supposed to protect them from the zombies. Many humans are killed, and their fearless leader, Kaufman, tries to get out of Dodge, but is confronted by zombie Cholo in the parking garage. To make matters worse for Kaufman, the zombie leader ends up blowing him up. These are fast-learning zombies!

When Dead Reckoning arrives at the city, it's too late to save people, so they basically try to blow up the place. Oddly, many of the poor people survive. I guess living in squalor isn't so bad during the apocalypse. While many of the survivors head in one direction, Riley and his crew head to Canada in Dead Reckoning. Interestingly, the zombies head in another direction, but Riley lets them go, figuring it's pointless to fight with them when they are just looking for their own space. This is a solid zombie flick, with a strong cast, but not in the must-see department.

Diary of the Dead (American, 2007)

Another respectable zombie film is *Diary of the Dead*, released in 2007, and written and directed by George Romero, "the zombie king." Like some of the better zombie flicks, this one clicked for me because of the interaction between an interesting cast of characters. We start out at the University of Pittsburg, where a group of students are making a horror movie about mummies for a film class. But the real story is about a guy who kills his wife and son before killing himself. You guessed it, they turn into zombies.

Now, once our student film crew find out about this, they decide to head home, but also to document what's happening "so people will know the truth"—well, mostly film student Jason Creed (Josh Close) does. He initially drives his girlfriend, Debra Moynihan (Michelle Morgan), crazy, along with everybody else, with his obsession of recording the events as they unfold. In any case, most of the group head out of town in an RV to get home. Their mummy actor Ridley Wilmott (Philip Riccio), and his girlfriend head off on their own to Ridley's home in suburban Philadelphia.

Our little group of survivors heads home, and they have more than their fair share of adventures. After running over a zombie, the RV driver, Mary (Tatiana Maslany), tries to kill herself, and after a quick visit to the hospital, the rest of the group lose her and another member of the group to a zombie attack. They move forward, and the next thing they know, they are trying to fix the RV in what appears to be an Amish area, but once again are attacked by zombies.

They manage to escape, but end up with a "close encounter" with some former National Guard members. Our rag-tag group of students has a rocky start with this group, but what can you expect in the apocalypse? However, Debra is able to convince the leader to give them the supplies they need to continue the trip. So it would appear all is well in "zombie land," but not quite. A group of paramilitary guys robs them, leaving them with only weapons, and their cameras, of course, to continue the story.

They eventually make it to Debra's home in Scranton, Pennsylvania, and connect with Debra's family. The bad news is that they are zombies. The group's next move is to head to Ridley's very large and very rich home, to find safety. Unfortunately, when they get there, things take a turn for the worse, as Ridley is already infected with the zombie virus, and informs our tiny band that his parents and everybody else are buried in the pool.

When Ridley turns, he chases Tracy (Amy Lalonde), who has been the group's mechanic and the most cheerful member of the group from the beginning. But, fed up with Ridley's advances, she drives off into the sunset. Meanwhile, Ridley kills one of the group, and then turns his attention toward Jason, our movie maker and documentarian, and manages to bite and infect him. Debra whacks Jason to prevent him from becoming a zombie, and then takes over his filming of the events. The three remaining survivors hole up in a safe room, wondering if mankind is worth saving after watching some of Jason's footage, as the film ends. Some might consider this film another formula zombie movie, but I thought it was a great story with a great cast. One worth watching!

Resident Evil (American, 2002)

There is no way I can escape commenting on the *Resident Evil* movie series, as it has certainly made a big splash with movie goers. However, I don't have to provide cover-to-cover coverage. The first installment was released in 2002, and appropriately called *Resident Evil*. This is one of those flicks where an evil corporation, the Umbrella Corporation, is doing some nasty genetic research underground in a place called the Hive, deep under Raccoon City. Probably to no one's surprise, the staff gets infected with something called the T-Virus, and trust me, this is not a good thing.

Well, as we soon discover, the T-Virus turns people into killer zombies, and the Umbrella Corporation is forced to send in a military team to take care of the problem. Along the way, they run into Alice (Milla Jovovich), the former head of security and now suffering from exposure to some kind of nerve gas. While they fight to contain the virus, they do not succeed and the virus escapes, infecting the outside world. Somehow Alice survives, but becomes another experiment for the Umbrella Corporation, and ends up in a coma and will need to deal with this mess in the next installment.

Resident Evil: Apocalypse (American, 2004)

OK, in the next chapter of this saga, *Resident Evil: Apocalypse* (2004), Alice awakens to find things have gone to hell. The virus has reached the surface, the police and military are losing control, and the city is about to be sealed off, leaving people to face bloodthirsty hordes of zombies without help. After Alice (Milla Jovovich) comes to her senses, she sets out for the city and hooks up with a small group, including police officer Jill Valentine (Sienna Guillory), Sergeant Peyton Wells (Razaaq Adoti), and a reporter. They join forces and try to fight their way out of trouble.

Unfortunately, they don't all make it. They lose Sergeant Wells and the reporter as they try to save the daughter of the Umbrella Corporation scientist who invented the T-Virus. While he may have helped them escape, I'm not sure why they bothered to help the guy who orchestrated the end of the world, but I didn't write the script.

Meanwhile, back at the ranch, the special forces people are getting their butts kicked by zombie hordes. One of the things I like about this movie is that there are different kinds of zombies. You've got your regular wackos, the genetically engineered variety, and the Umbrella Corp's candidate for the zombie of the year award, Nemesis, which is their version of a super zombie. Word of advice, stay away. Even Alice has been genetically tampered with. Another interesting part of this film is that this is the first time I've seen a class of zombie kids, which our little crew encounters when they are rescuing the mad scientist's daughter.

Well, when you have a corrupt corporation out of control, genetically modified zombies running all over the place, and a super zombie to contend with, only one thing can happen. A fight to the finish! However, while Alice is trying to take on Nemesis, she realizes he is a mutated Matt Addison from an earlier encounter in the Hive, and refuses to kill him. He is touched, and they both take on the forces of the Umbrella Corporation. Alice ends up badly wounded as she tries to save the scientist's daughter. Not to worry, they made a lot of money on this flick, so our pals at the Umbrella Corporation take Alice away for some more experimentation, and she gets to fight another day in the next movie.

Resident Evil: Extinction (American, 2007)

My final contribution to the *Resident Evil* series is *Resident Evil: Extinction*, released in 2007. The reason I'm covering this occasionally confusing third installment in the series is because the T-Virus has finally trashed the world. Our genetically modified hero, Alice (Milla Jovovich), who is actually a clone, is stuck in a mansion fighting to get out, but never succeeding. The real Alice is off playing *Easy Rider* in the desert, fighting zombie dogs and anything else that gets in her way.

Eventually the real Alice hooks up with a caravan of survivors who are looking for supplies. Unfortunately, some of the group gets picked off, and the entire unit is attacked by zombie crows, also infected by the T-Virus. Along the way, someone decides the group should head for Alaska. Apparently, zombies don't like the cold. Meanwhile, back at the Umbrella Corporation, the leadership is still trying to figure out how to control the world. Given the state of the world, it's not clear why that's worth the effort. But they are trying to find a cure, and their zombie domestication program has taught some how to use cell phones. Too bad they still crave human flesh and try to devour their teachers. The former CEO of Umbrella, Dr. Isaacs (Iain Glen), actually manages to get infected, but becomes some kind of super zombie who can use tentacles to destroy anything in his way.

Alice discovers her blood is the actual cure for the T-Virus, but she has to deal with the transformed Isaacs in a battle of the century. Is there any doubt who wins? After taking care of Isaacs, she sends a message to other branches of the Umbrella Corporation that she is coming for them, and in the next scene you see that scores of cloned Alices are being prepared for that assignment. This is an entertaining movie, but the third installment is about all I can handle. Despite a really good cast and a decent plot, this story could have been told in two episodes. Getting through the third movie was a little tedious, but that didn't stop them from making others.

Zombie Apocalypse (American, 2011)

As we stroll down zombie memory lane, we cannot but help stumble on *Zombie Apocalypse*, released in 2011. To call this film mediocre would be a bit generous, but I have always been a fan of Ving Rhames, who was great in the 2004 remake of *Dawn of the Dead*.

We all know how bad those zombie plagues can be, and this one is no exception, wiping out 90% of the population in six months. But there are bands of survivors out there looking for some "safe spaces." Two groups end up joining forces, and they decide to head for Catalina Island, which is one of those safe havens. How many times have we heard about safe places in zombie movies? In any case, one of their team gets bitten and has to be taken out, but the rest march on. This flick seems to have both fast and slow zombies, which I have always found intellectually challenging. I mean, if you're dead, how fast can you do the hundred? Well, they head to a local high school to take refuge, but zombies have overrun the place and they lose another member of their group. After fighting their way to the coast, they arrive at the place where the boat is supposed to pick up survivors to take them to Catalina. The bad news is that there are a couple of what appear to be infected tigers, which attack the group. Henry (Ving Rhames) has a battle with one and saves the female lead, Cassie (Lesley-Ann Brandt), but dies in the process.

The closing scene shows what's left of our little band waiting on the dock as the boat heads toward them. This flick is hardly at the top of the list, and the script is all too predictable and kind of stale. But the infected tigers were a nice twist, and no complaints about the cast.

Autumn (Canadian, 2009)

In the "little" movie category, but not on my must-see list, is the Canadian film *Autumn* (2009). Once again, some kind of virus kills off most of the human race, and the movie focuses on how a few survive. For the most part, it's about three survivors. There were a few more, including a guy in a clown costume, but three set out to find an isolated place to stay in the country to improve their chances, and get away from rotting corpses.

Now, this is, in effect, another zombie movie, but these zombies go through a kind of evolution. They start out as dopey clods that can't get out of their own way. But as time goes on, they get nastier, and become the type of zombies we know and love. When they ate a little dog, I knew things were getting out of hand. One of our three survivors heads off on his own, and decides to hang out with David Carradine for a little bit. But David is a bit off and doesn't want to leave his zombie mom. I think David Carradine died the same year this film was released, and I'm hoping the two events are not connected. Anyway, our third survivor heads back to his friends, and then sacrifices himself to save his two friends. This film has got David Carradine, a clown zombie, a small band trying to survive, but that's about it. Not much soul, and not on any top-ten list.

World War Z (American, 2013)

Now, *World War Z* (2013) is a film that comes very late to the zombie and post-apocalyptic film genres (close to fifty years after *Night of the Living Dead*), but, nevertheless, is an excellent film. I think it's zombie storytelling at its best. The cause of the zombie virus is not that new, but the process of dealing with it is fairly imaginative. Also, the special effects were really cool, but they didn't overwhelm the story and characters.

The film stars Brad Pitt as former U.N. worker Gerry Lane, Mireille Enos as his wife Karin, Daniella Kertesz as Israeli soldier Segen, and David Morse as a rather far-out former CIA agent. The film starts out with the Lanes and their two daughters enjoying an idyllic family breakfast. But the next thing you know they are stuck in Philadelphia traffic, where a zombie outbreak occurs. There is some great aerial photography in these scenes as zombies overrun the city. Gerry and Karin try to get their family out, and steal an RV in the process. After talking to Gerry's former boss at the U.N., Thierry Umutoni (Fana Mokoena), the family heads to Newark, New Jersey, for safety.

Now I'm not sure Newark would be at the top of my list for safe places, but Gerry's boss tells him they will pick him up in the morning on the rooftop of a tall building. Unfortunately, the building they chose is not zombie proof, and they have to be saved by another family in the building. While Gerry tries to convince the father to allow Gerry to take his family with them to escape, the father refuses, and, sadly, the zombies kill all but his young son. After a narrow rooftop escape, the Lane family ends up on an aircraft carrier off the coast.

It looks like the family will be safe—but not so fast. The U.N. has plans for Gerry. Bottom line, if he doesn't join an effort to go to South Korea to find Patient Zero (the first person infected) and a cure, he and his family will get kicked off the boat. So Gerry is off to South Korea. While the doctor supposed to cure the problem ends up shooting himself, Gerry gets some useful intelligence from a former CIA agent, who tells him the Israelis knew this was coming and built a wall to protect themselves. So, it's off to Israel, where Gerry talks with Jurgen Warmbrunn (Ludi Boeken), the head of Israeli defenses. Once there, he finds out the rather complex logic to the Israeli defenses against the zombies, which can probably be best described as "let's do it just in case," and the hopelessness of finding the original person who was infected. Because these zombies are attracted to noise (aren't they always), Jerusalem, too, gets overrun because of the racket they are making in the process of saving people.

Lane is joined by an Israeli soldier, Segen, who tries to help him escape. Unfortunately, she gets bitten, and Lane has to chop her hand off to try to save her. And it works! Then they board a plane to get out of Jerusalem as it's overrun. This is an incredibly effective sequence in the film; you can almost feel the anxiety of the passengers on that plane as they see zombies coming at them from all over. The plane sequence itself is also incredible, as zombies take over the plane until Lane actually brings the plane down with a grenade. However, before that happens, Lane gets the pilot to fly them to the nearest World Health Organization facility. Even though the plane crashes, Lane and Segen make it there.

So why does Lane want to go there? Well, along the way, he saw how zombies completely bypassed some people while they went after others. Lane presumes these are sick people, and I guess zombies don't like to eat sick people. While they may not be able to cure the zombie virus, Lane figures that by infecting people with serious illnesses for which they have a cure, they have a better chance of fighting off the zombies. To test this theory, Lane infects himself with some really bad stuff, and guess what, the zombies leave him alone.

They make a vaccine to be given to those fighting zombies, which finally gives them a chance. Meanwhile, Gerry is reunited with his family at a safe zone in Nova Scotia, and there is hope, but the film lets you know the war isn't over yet. This is a great film, and in my top three all-time best zombie movies.

Extinction (American, 2015)

In 2015, Vertical Entertainment released the film *Extinction*. What makes this film interesting is that we start out with regular zombies, but after about nine years they seem to evolve into more adaptive creatures. For the record though, they still want to eat humans.

OK, after another one of those zombie viruses, survivors get on a couple of school buses to get out of Dodge. However, they get attacked by zombies anyway, and things go bad. No surprise there. The folks on the second bus try to escape, and that includes our main guys, Patrick (Matthew Fox) and Jack (Jeffrey Donavan). Oh, and they take baby girl Lu (Quinn McColgan). Kind of like *Three Men and a Baby*, but the zombies got the third guy.

While Patrick is Lu's biological father, she ends up living with Jack, whom she calls Dad. Patrick and Jack have a falling out, mostly because Patrick is a drunk and can't be trusted to take care of Lu. They even live separately. Nine years go by, and they fall into their routines, basically acting like zombies are a thing of the past. They are wrong, and soon Patrick is attacked by one of the infected, who seem physically different—leaner and faster—than the original zombies.

While Patrick tries to warn Jack about what's happening, Patrick's dog is the one who saves him. Even though he gets bitten, it seems Patrick may be immune. Lu is angry with Jack for not doing enough to save Patrick. Jack goes along with Lu to invite Patrick over for dinner, and the two men try to repair their relationship. Soon afterwards they find a woman who somehow managed to survive a zombie attack. On a supply run, they find a woman in distress, and take her home with them, but realize the zombies will be coming for them.

Apparently, these zombies howl to each other to communicate. The survivors board up the house to protect themselves, but it turns out to be a losing battle, as their generator runs out of gas. Patrick decides to make the noble sacrifice and draw the infected away from the other three, allowing them time to get away. So Jack, Lu, and the woman drive off into the sunset, while poor Patrick gets taken out by zombies. In a final act of defiance, Patrick blows himself up, and takes out a bunch of zombies in the process. I guess this is as close as you get to a happy ending in a zombie apocalypse.

This is certainly an OK flick, with a good cast and a decent story, but hardly at the top of my zombie list. If you want to spend a couple of hours watching a zombie movie, go for one of the big three: *Night of the Living Dead*, *Dawn of the Dead*, or *World War Z*.

Collapse (American, 2011)

If anybody has any doubt that post-apocalyptic zombie films are a cottage industry, you only have to watch *Collapse*, released in 2011. The good news is that these films often give some talented actors a chance to practice their craft, and if they have a halfway decent script, these flicks can be enjoyable. In the case of *Collapse*, we are batting around .500. The main character is Robert Morgan, played by Chris Mulkey, who is a fine actor. Karen Landry plays his wife, Molly Morgan, the other main character.

Robert is a financially troubled farmer in a small town when it appears that all hell breaks loose. All of a sudden, zombies start showing up at his farm, infecting his son and a farm hand. He kills the farm hand and tries to help treat his son. He barricades his family in his home, and tries to figure out what's happening. Meanwhile, some more zombies show up, and his supplies start to run out. He decides he must make a run into town to get what they need, but his wife pleads with him not to go. Go he must, but when he gets to town—surprise, surprise—there are more zombies there. Lucky for him they are the ambling kind, and not very fast.

Perhaps one of the high points of the film—and this should tell you something—is that he finds a zombie head in the sink, snarling at him. Robert didn't like the guy in life, so he gives him the business, and even keeps the head for a spell. As he tries to collect supplies, he finds a woman hiding in a store, and urges her to come home with him. However, she opens the bag with the head and gets bitten, and poor Robert ends up shooting her.

Now some real drama kicks in, and you start to realize this isn't a real zombie apocalypse but Robert going a little wacko, probably from mounting pressures on him, and from killing people. In one of the final scenes, you see a horde of zombies headed toward his farm, and see them evaporate as police cars drive through them to stop Robert from killing more people.

Unfortunately, Robert is too far gone to stop, and he starts shooting at the police, too, who are really zombies in his eyes. He even tries to kill his wife, whom he imagines is also a zombie. The film ends with police trying to subdue a wounded Robert, who sees them as attacking him. It's an interesting little movie that, up till the last ten minutes of the film, really had only a couple of speaking parts. An interesting flick, and Chis Milkey does a very good job with the role, but not on any must-see list.

Pandemic (American, 2016)

I kind of liked the film *Pandemic*, released in 2016, which represents an interesting little virus-type movie that flows fairly well for a low budget flick. In this film, the viewer gets a taste of zombie evolution, as the undead go through five levels of zombiedom! You start out as mildly infected and treatable, through level five when you become a raving maniac. The film starts out just after a worldwide pandemic where most of the human population is wiped out. So what else is new! Of course, they don't tell you why—for all I know it started with a bad batch of fries at Mickey D's.

Well, we bring in Dr. Lauren Chase (Rachel Nichols) and a small team to retrieve some survivors holed up at a school. She isn't really a doctor, as we find out later, but checking medical credentials during a zombie apocalypse isn't what it should be. Lauren is really looking for her daughter, whom she left behind in LA while she was on a business trip to New York. Too bad that happened during the outbreak.

The team doesn't have much luck retrieving survivors, but Lauren does find and bring back her daughter. Unfortunately, the zombies pick off everyone else on her team, but she does get her mildly infected daughter back to the compound. Mom is no dummy and realizes her daughter will only be accepted at the compound if they think it is really her, so she puts her uniform on her daughter, and while Lauren gets shot when they reach the compound, her daughter is admitted. This is a totally decent effort in the zombie genre.

Here Alone (American, 2016)

Perhaps more of a pseudo-zombie film rather than a real zombie film is *Here Alone*, released in 2016. The reason for this is that there aren't many zombies around in this one. In fact, there are not that many people around, either. I guess the title should be your first clue. This is another one of those little low budget post-apocalyptic films that starts out with one of those viruses that wipes out most of humanity.

While the basic plot offers nothing all that new, the cast, especially Lucy Walters, who plays Ann, does a great job and is very convincing. Still, I found this film a little tedious at times, and kind of stale. We start our post-apocalyptic saga with Ann and her husband and baby heading for the hills—or more specifically, the woods—after a viral outbreak. The story about Ann's family is basically told in flashbacks, while the current focus is on how Ann survives. I thought this was the best part of the film.

Along the way, Ann shows her humanity and helps an injured man, Chris (Adam David Thomson), and his stepdaughter, Olivia (Gina Piersanti). In between flashback reminiscences, our little group tries to develop trust as they try to survive and forage for food. Perhaps one of the more interesting scenes is a zombie getting taken out with what appears to be a non-headshot. I don't think I have ever seen that before in the genre. While Chris and Olivia want to move on, they never really make it. On a food run, Ann and Olivia get separated, and when Olivia returns to Chris, he thinks the worst has happened. At that time, a group of zombies attacks the pair and Chris is killed fighting them off. In the next scene, you see the two women driving off into the zombie sunset. This is hardly a great one, but if you have an hour and a half to use up, be my guest.

Zombieland (American, 2009)

If you need some relief from the pressures of post-apocalyptic movies, I can suggest some post-apocalyptic light. *Zombieland*, released in 2009, is just what the doctor ordered. This mix of a neurotic zombie hunter, a Twinkie addict, a couple of female con artists, and a former Saturday Night Live host make for a really fun apocalypse. The cast includes Jessie Eisenberg, Woody Harrelson, Emma Stone, Abigail Breslin, and Bill Murray.

After an outbreak of "mad zombie disease," the United States becomes Zombieland, and not a nice place to visit. We start our saga with a wimpy college kid named Columbus (Jessie Eisenberg) who, before the apocalypse, has as his biggest problem finding a girlfriend. While he does find the girl of his dreams, she turns into a zombie and tries to devour him. Now, one thing you can say about Columbus, he is a careful guy. He comes up with a list of how to deal with the zombie apocalypse: things like shoot a zombie twice, "double tap," just to make sure are dead. In any case, Columbus decides to return home to see if his family is still alive, and manages to connect with Tallahassee (Woody Harrelson), a Twinkie-loving, zombie-hating, gun-toting redneck.

Reluctantly, Tallahassee agrees to travel with Columbus, and the two then meet two young women, Wichita (Emma Stone) and Little Rock (Abigail Breslin), who manage to steal their guns and car. Well, they find a new car and more guns, and manage to reconnect with the two female con artists, and, after a few tense moments, they all decide to try to survive together. Columbus has a crush on Wichita, and actually tries to impress her in a rather feeble way, but more importantly, they all decide to head west.

Somehow, they make it to Bill Murray's mansion in Hollywood, but Columbus accidently shoots him, thinking he's a zombie. They do give Bill a nice funeral, wrapping him up in a sheet and throwing him over the roof. Well, it seems Wichita is getting attracted to Columbus, but decides to run off, with Little Rock in tow, to avoid any commitments. Columbus convinces Tallahassee to go after them, and the four meet up at a place called Pacific Playland, where they engage in a massive battle against a zombie horde. Not only do they survive the battle, but boy gets girl, Tallahassee gets a Twinkie, and the four head off into the zombie sunset as one big happy family. This film is fun to watch, and represents some really good storytelling.

Chapter Nine: TV Apocalypse

"Alas, Babylon," Playhouse 90 (American, 1960)

The big screen isn't the only place for post-apocalyptic entertainment. TV has made a contribution, too. In fact, as in the movies, there has been an explosion of series that deal with this subject over the past 8–10 years. One of the most significant chapters in my fascination with this subject began on television. The title of this show was "Alas, Babylon," and it first appeared on the old *Playhouse 90* show. The story was based on the incredible novel by Pat Frank, which I have read at least twice. According to IMDb, the show aired April 3, 1960, and to the best of my knowledge, I only saw it once, but I have scoured sci-fi conventions trying to find a copy. This program and *Panic in Year Zero* are the two films that really helped create my interest in this genre more than any other productions.

Since I saw this a long time ago, but have read the novel a couple of times, they kind of blur together in my mind. The episode had an incredible cast for a TV program, including Dana Andrews (*Best Years of Our Lives*), Don Murray (*Hoodlum Priest*), Kim Hunter (*Planet of the Apes*), Rita Moreno (*West Side Story*), Burt Reynolds (*Smokey and the Bandit*), Barbara Rush (*Come Blow Your Horn*), Don Gordon (*Bullitt*), and Everett Sloane (*Somebody Up There Likes Me*). Wow, this is one impressive group of actors!

Well, considering when the book was written and when the program aired, nuclear war is once again the culprit in this post-apocalyptic story. The story takes place in a small town in Florida called Fort Repose. Two of the principal characters are Mark and Randy Bragg (Dana Andrews and Don Murray). Since Mark is in the military, he gets wind of a coming disaster and informs his brother with a telegram, using the words "Alas Babylon," which means bad shit is going down.

It looks like the Cold War is over and both sides launch nuclear weapons after a mistaken bombing somewhere in the Middle East. Not surprisingly, things go from bad to worse as people try to cope with the after-effects.

Perhaps one of the more interesting aspects of this type of film is how people cope with their "New World." Randy Bragg helps organize the community to ensure food and water get to people, and they get rid of any radioactive stuff. As months go by, it's clear there is not much of a government left, and they are basically on their own. The president is now some former junior secretary of basket weaving, and things look bleak. However, our little town of Fort Repose continues to hang in there, and when the Air Force offers to evacuate them about a year later, they decide to stay. This is a great flick that every "doomsday prepper" should see.

"Atomic Attack," The Motorola Television Hour (American, 1954)

Almost by accident, and thanks to Amazon Prime, I recently discovered a TV show episode called "Atomic Attack," which was an episode of *The Motorola Television Hour*, first shown in 1954. The show seems dated, but was well acted, with a cast that included Phyllis Thaxter and Walter Matthau. After your typical all-American family breakfast, followed by Dad headed for work and the kids off to school, Mom's chores are interrupted by a nuclear attack on New York City. The family lives about 50 miles from the city, and while they miss the impact of the blast, the fallout headed their way will affect them.

This is truly a Cold War kind of propaganda-type film in that it makes it abundantly clear that we are kicking the enemy's ass (enemy unnamed), and the government has things under control. Nevertheless, the fear that Mom and her two daughters feel is real and powerful. The show does present some of the usual things you would expect to see in nuclear war, such as radiation sickness, looting, people trying to help others, and outright fear. Yet it almost seems the show didn't want to scare people too much. While Dad gets fried in NYC, and the younger daughter gets radiation sickness, people don't seem all that concerned about resources, and in some ways, life goes on as normal. In fact, the show does suggest that things will get better, and despite the hardship, there is still a future.

Although the show seems dated, it has to be considered a groundbreaking effort. As far as I can figure, this is the first of its kind, and it debuted a full six years before "Alas, Babylon." It may be only the second film or TV show to address the realities of nuclear war directly, preceded only by the film *Five*. Of course, my comments might be U.S.-centric as I am not aware of what other countries produced along these lines. If you have the time, it's worth a watch.

"Time Enough At Last," The Twilight Zone (American, 1959)

The Twilight Zone had a few episodes with end-of-the-world themes. But one in particular stands out for me, "Time Enough At Last," staring Burgess Meredith. For all practical purposes, this is almost a one-man show for Meredith, who plays the bookish and henpecked Henry Bemis. All Henry wants to do is read, but his wife and boss are determined to break that habit. Nevertheless, Henry takes his lunch in a bank vault one day when a nuclear holocaust happens. Everybody is wiped out but poor old Henry. Henry is distraught to find himself alone in the world, and even considers taking his own life. But then he discovers the library, and a hopeful Henry Bemis plans all the books he is going to read. Unfortunately, Henry is very nearsighted, and while trying to pick up something, his glasses fall and break. Henry's response is, "It's just not fair." So, there isn't even any justice in the apocalypse.

"The Midnight Sun," The Twilight Zone (American, 1961)

Another *Twilight Zone* episode that was even more imaginative is "The Midnight Sun," which aired on November 17, 1961. This episode tells the story of two women living in a New York City apartment building as the Earth leaves its orbit, heading toward the sun. Temperatures are rising, power is dwindling, and water is becoming a precious commodity. The two women, Norma (Lois Nettleson) and Mrs. Bronson (Betty Garde), struggle to survive in a building that is just about empty except for them. All the neighbors have moved north, trying to avoid the heat. The two women try to help each other, and both get a fright when an intruder breaks in looking to loot the building. He gets into their apartment, and while he seems scary at first, he is just a poor soul who lost his family and has been made desperate by the heat. He even begs their forgiveness, and then leaves. Meanwhile, the temperature is rising, so high that Norma's paintings start to melt. But then the plot changes. Norma has been ill and suffering from a high fever, but when the fever breaks, we see a snowstorm, not the sun. We now learn that, indeed, the Earth has moved from its orbit, but it is moving *away* from the sun, not towards it. In either case, mankind is screwed.

"Two," The Twilight Zone (American, 1961)

The Twilight Zone was a wonderful show that holds up well almost 60 years after the first episode. To be honest, it has always been one of my favorite TV shows. I have a complete set of the series, and never miss the TV marathons of the show. In any case, there are a couple of additional episodes I want to mention. The first is "Two," which is the opening episode for season three. It stars Charles Bronson and Elizabeth Montgomery as two soldiers on opposing sides after a great war. This episode aired about three years before Montgomery starred in her own show, *Bewitched*.

Both characters in this installment of the *Twilight Zone* appear worn out and disheveled. I think viewers are expected to understand that they don't speak the same language, because only Charles Bronson's character talks. However, you do get the impression Montgomery understands him. Now, after the devastation of this great war, you expect even soldiers to be weary of any additional fighting. Bronson's character is fed up, and wants no part of any additional fighting. Montgomery's character may feel the same way, but she still is distrustful and has an itchy trigger finger. Despite the fact that he shares food with her, and smashes a window to get her a nice dress, she still tries to shoot him. Maybe she thought the dress was a sexist gesture, and that was payback. Interestingly, despite the fact they may be the last two people on Earth, they are still trying to kill one another. Well, Bronson has had enough of her and walks away. The next day he cleans himself up and puts on a new suit, and as he gets ready to leave the dumpy town he was in, he sees the woman wearing the dress he gave her. They smile at each other and then walk away together. Another *Twilight Zone* classic and, despite the horrible impact of a devastating war, it ends with hope!

"The Old Man in the Cave," The Twilight Zone (American, 1963)

The final *Twilight Zone* episode I will cover aired in November 1963 (season 5) and was called "The Old Man in the Cave." The show begins in a small town in 1974, which is ten years after a horrible nuclear war. The town has become dependent on an old man in a nearby cave, and his spokesman, Mr. Goldsmith (John Anderson, a regular in the *Twilight Zone* series). The town is trying to find out if some canned food they found is safe to eat. Goldsmith tells them the old man says the food is contaminated and should be destroyed.

Well, to the starving townspeople that isn't a popular call, but a small group of soldiers come to the rescue, headed by a scruffy-looking officer, Major French (James Coburn). These so-called soldiers are really a bunch of bullies who survive by looting and taking from others. But they convince the townspeople the food is OK to eat. And by the way, who is this old man to decide everything for them? Stirring up the townspeople, French has them break into the cave, where they find out the old man is really a computer. Well, they decide the hell with the old man and eat the food. You guessed it, the food was contaminated, and they all die, including the soldiers. The only survivor is Mr. Goldsmith. It's hardly a happy ending, but not surprising, either. This episode offers no hope, and despite the limitations of a one-hour TV show, captures the bleak realities of a world devastated by nuclear war.

Where Have All the People Gone? (American, 1974)

In 1974, at the height of the "disaster movie" craze, ABC debuted a TV movie called *Where Have All the People Gone?* It had a fairly imaginative plot, which had most of humanity being taken out by solar flares. The cast included Peter *"Mission Impossible"* Graves, Verna Bloom, and Kathleen Quinlan. While it started out well, it quickly became a typically sterile made-for-TV movie. Steven Anders (Graves) and his two children survive while on vacation, and he spends most of the rest of the film trying to get home to his wife.

You know, in post-apocalyptic movies at least half of the survivors are bad or evil, and that's true here, too, but you don't see many. However, an accountant does almost take out Graves as they are searching for food. Rather embarrassing! Graves and his children pick up a couple of people along the way: a little boy and a woman who was traumatized by the loss of her family. Apparently, dogs ate her kids. I am not kidding.

Well, they finally make it home, only to find that Graves's wife is dead. Believe it or not, it seems that survivors have a gene that gives them immunity from solar flares, and I'm guessing his wife didn't have that gene. OK, you don't buy it; take it up with the writers.

The woman they picked up is still so upset that she tries to drown herself, but Peter Graves reminds her they have to go on. And go on they do, to Northern California, where they can all start over. I give the film credit for coming up with a new idea—how many times has humanity been destroyed by solar flares?—but that's about it. The film also deserves credit for an early attempt to show the effects of a failure of the power grid. You can see the movie for free on the Internet if you have a mind to. Bring plenty of coffee if you plan to sit through it.

Threads (British, 1984)

The next three films I would like to mention are all made-for-TV films that were done in the 1980s, and all are about nuclear war. My recollection is that the British film *Threads*, a docudrama, had the most compelling message, and not surprisingly, was the most depressing. The Brits are good that way! The focus is on realism, not development of various characters, and even watching the trailer on YouTube recently still made me cringe. People getting burnt and blown apart is not particularly pleasant. Unlike other films, I saw this one purely as a warning to mankind.

While the film provides stats and updates about the war's impact on the world, Sheffield, England, is the primary focus. However, the human part of the story begins with two young people; Ruth Beckett and Jimmy Kemp are getting ready to marry as a result of an unplanned pregnancy. But a nuclear war puts the kibosh on that. Instead, like the rest of the residents of Sheffield, they must struggle to survive.

Talk about a crap storm, but Sheffield has to deal with collapsing buildings that trap many people, radiation sickness, people suffering from severe burns, no food or water, and limited sanitation. Martial law is declared, and capital punishment is brought back to deal with criminals who are preying on others. Things go from bad to worse, as diseases start to spread.

Through all this, Ruth gives birth to a daughter, Jane, and manages to live for another ten years, but ends up dead in a field. While things are starting to get better, Jane, still a child herself, gives birth to a still-born child. Make no mistake; this is a very powerful anti-war film that just happens to fit into the post-apocalyptic category. From my point of view, it was more designed to warn rather than entertain.

Testament (American, 1983)

Across the pond, two American TV films came out on the subject of nuclear war. I enjoyed both films, and while they were powerful indictments of nuclear war, neither was quite as grim as *Threads,* but they weren't far behind. *Testament* and *The Day After* were both produced in 1983, and both were graced with strong casts and good scripts. In fact, *Testament,* which was made as a TV movie, actually had a brief theatrical release because the filmmaker thought it was that good. Nevertheless, it ended up on TV, and that's where I saw it.

In *Testament,* the story more or less centers around the Wetherly family, which consists of Tom (William Devane), Carol (Jane Alexander), and their kids. Tom works in San Francisco, so you don't hear much about him, given what happens. In any case, Jane Alexander is with her kids. One of the youngest is watching TV when news reports suddenly appear indicating the East Coast has been hit by nuclear weapons. Well, this family lives in a small town outside San Francisco, but the bombs make it there, too. The good news is that they are far enough from San Francisco to not suffer the usual fate of nuclear war. At least not right away!

Well, people may be scared out of their wits, and rightly so. The town tries to function as normally as possible. Hell, even a school play goes on as scheduled. The show must go on! The bad news is that radiation poisoning starts taking its toll. The film is quite effective in demonstrating the devastating effects of radiation, as it starts killing off people in the town, and essentially reducing the town to a chaotic state. Carol loses her son, Scottie; a young couple loses an infant child; and essential services break down. Carol even decides to have her family commit suicide, but can't go through with it. They have a birthday party instead, and you see a family movie celebrating Tom's birthday closing out the film. Jane Alexander gives an awesome performance as Carol, and really makes the film. It's powerful and, like *Threads*, it can scare the hell out of you.

The Day After (American, 1983)

The Day After and *Testament* have sometimes blurred together for me, so it was helpful to view them both recently again. They were released the same year, and cover basically the same subject; only the locations are different. *Testament* takes place in a small town in California; in *The Day After,* we are in Kansas and Missouri—more specifically, Lawrence, Kansas. As is often the case in these flicks, the Soviet Union is up to its old tricks. After some kind of troop rebellion of the East Germans, the Soviets turn up the heat, and after ultimatums are made and ignored, we end up in a nuclear war.

What I liked about the movie was the nice little town that people in the movie lived in. Andy and Opie of Mayberry would love the place, and it looks like an ideal place to have a life. During the first 30 minutes of the movie, I wanted to move there. There's one downside though: you have a bunch of missile silos nearby that can do a number on the landscape when used. In a scene where the U.S. launches its missiles, you can see lines of smoke all over the area as the missiles head to their targets. This is a very effective sequence, and more than a little scary. I think this is the first time I saw an electromagnetic pulse (EMP) in a movie. The film also provides scenes where people are burned and vaporized. There is a church scene in this film that is particularly heart-breaking. The painful delivery of the preacher's sermon to a flock that is devastated and sick in his bombed-out church is gut-wrenching.

In this film, you follow the transition of key characters who go from normal lives to total devastation. Jason Robards, as Dr. Russell Oakes, is a very sympathetic figure who works tirelessly to save lives, even though he is suffering from radiation sickness. Unlike *Testament*, in this film you watch radiation sickness slowly consume the characters. *Testament* is much less visual in this respect. John Callum plays a farmer who fights a losing battle to hold his family together. As the film progresses, radiation sickness seems to affect just about everyone. As expected, society breaks down and there is plenty of looting, violence, and even a few executions. But people do try to help each other, too. In one of the closing scenes, Jason Robards shares an embrace with a squatter who is living in what's left of his house. Unlike *Threads*, where Jane gives birth to a stillborn child, Amy Madigan's character gives birth to a healthy child. Perhaps there is hope for us after all.

These three movies (*Threads*, *Testament*, *The Day After*), more than others of this kind, made the reality of nuclear war in all its gruesome detail something to think about and fear. After watching them, one has to wonder why anyone would make such weapons. You can chalk up WWII efforts to inexperience, but how can you explain the lack of wisdom in continuing the stockpiling process of these weapons? Like the floating fallout in *On the Beach* (1959), the stuff eventually gets everybody. In fact, you can drop all your nuclear bombs on yourselves, and know everybody else in the world will share the same fate. At the end of *The Day After*, a posted message warns our leaders that if they don't want this to happen, they'd better find a more peaceful way to live.

Jericho (American, 2006)

Since we are on the subject of nuclear war, the next TV show to discuss is *Jericho*. Season One first appeared in September 2006 and didn't do too well, but the show managed to last until 2008. This is one I watched fairly recently, but threw in the towel after six episodes. They had a good cast, but this thing played out like a soap opera. It was like the end of the world meets *Cheers*. Despite nuclear bombs going off nearby, and all kinds of bad stuff happening, they still managed to keep the local bar open 24/7.

The story centers on the fictional town of Jericho, Kansas. You can see nuclear bombs exploding and rockets being launched, which made the first two installments engaging, but that's about it. Sure, they show people trying to get their lives in order, and cope with the aftermath of nuclear war. But it lacked the soul and conviction of movies like *Testament* and *The Day After*.

Without Warning (American, 1994)

If nuclear war continued to be a popular post-apocalyptic theme in the 1980s, "cosmic crap" became popular in the 1990s. In the 1994 TV docudrama *Without Warning*, asteroids and aliens combine to do in humanity. The movie stars Sander Vanocur (playing himself) as a TV journalist reporting on some heavy-duty meteors threatening Earth. The entire story is done as a news report. You know, "We interrupt this program to report" that a giant meteor is about to fall on your head. By the way, we are going to throw in a couple of earthquakes, too.

Additionally, it appears that three big meteors are headed our way and they can cause the destruction of our planet. Not to worry, the military steps in, and after some close calls, manages to take out the meteors. Earth is saved; well, maybe not. We soon find out that, for reasons not explained, aliens are behind this mess, and they are sending a lot more crap our way. As Sander is reporting, parts of the Earth are being wiped off the map. He informs us he will stay on till the end, and even manages to quote Shakespeare. Talk about good ratings! Well, I would have been more impressed if Sander had said, "I'm getting the hell out of here," but that's just me. This is one of those films that are available on YouTube if you want to watch for free. Remember, you get what you pay for.

Asteroid vs Earth (American, 2014)

Now, most of us know that made-for-TV movies do not always deliver quality films. They sometimes try to imitate better films, but with a much lower budget. I would categorize our next film, *Asteroid vs Earth* (2014), as the poor man's *Deep Impact* or *Armageddon*. You can guess by the title that the world is headed for an extinction-level event as a result of the impact of a massive meteor headed directly at Earth. Now, of course, the army is called in, and they are ready with the nukes, but a smart Asian-American kid tells them it would be better to move the world than blow up the meteor. Not sure I would go for this, but this is certainly a new approach.

They try to get the Russians and Chinese to help, and have guys running all over the place to get nukes in the right place at the right time. Premature attempts to blow the meteor off course end up breaking a large piece off, and now it's bye-bye, Hong Kong. A key to getting this plan to work is to have a nuclear sub deliver its nukes in an ocean trench at the right time. You also need a guy to drop a couple of nukes into a volcano, which he does, and goes in with them. Now, you know our sub is going to face challenges, too. I understand they had to lose the captain, but did they have to blow the sub in half to pull it off? Well, I guess they did, because mankind is saved. This is a typical low budget TV movie: mildly entertaining, but not very compelling.

The Stand (American, 1994)

A somewhat disappointing TV series that was released in 1994 was Steven King's *The Stand*. This TV mini-series had a cast that consisted of a who's who of 1980s actors, such as Gary Sinise, Molly Ringwald, and Rob Lowe. The cast also included Ruby Dee, Ozzie Davis, and Ray Walston.

The plot starts out simply enough; those crazy government guys accidently let loose a deadly virus that kills off most of the human race. I wish those guys would stop playing around with that crap, but what can you do, it was in the script. Now, the plot thickens, as survivors start to have dreams about one of two people: an old woman or a very scary dude. In the dreams, survivors are encouraged to go to a place in Nebraska, where they meet the kindly Mother Abigail (Ruby Dee), or to Las Vegas to join Randall Flagg (Jamey Sheridan). Take a guess who the bad guy is; yup, that would be Randall. And he is basically a proxy for the devil. So the good people go to Mother Abigail, and the rest go to Flagg.

Basically, and rather simplistically, this evolves into a kind of religious war between good and evil. Despite all kinds of trials and tribulations, in the end, the good guys win. Of course, it doesn't hurt when some wacked-out disease-infected guy called Trashcan Man detonates a nuclear bomb in Vegas, which takes out Flagg and all his followers. Now the good guys get a chance to rebuild the world.

Despite a talented cast, this series was slow moving and rather shallow. Frankly, it was very hard to get into. My concentration often waned (I had to go back to my notes), except in the early segments.

Survivors (British, 2008)

The next installment of our saga is the BBC production *Survivors*. It was a well scripted series, had a wonderful cast, yet the BBC saw fit to kill it after 12 episodes. I will never forgive them for that, and they took a lot of heat from the fan base on this one. In any case, the series was originally released in 2008, with a second season in 2010, and was set in the present day. Unlike the previous series we have discussed, this post-apocalyptic world is not the result of nuclear war but a virus. I think they called it the European Flu, which kills off about 90% of the population. This virus is similar to the 1918 Spanish Flu, but far more deadly.

The story focuses on an unlikely group of survivors who band together to ride out the apocalypse. At the center of this motley crew is Abby Grant (Julie Graham). She is basically the uncrowned leader of the group, and the only one who actually survived the flu. If you are ever stuck in a post-apocalyptic situation, you want to have Abby with you. Other cast members include Tom Price (Max Beesley), Greg Preston (Paterson Joseph), Anya Raczynski (Zoe Rhys), and Aalim Sadiq (Philip Rhys). The group doesn't always get along, but they do act like a family, even if a little dysfunctional.

Well, this whole mess starts with a virus or flu that essentially destroys civilization—you know, contamination, no electricity, chaos, looting, and limited food supplies. At the outset of this mess, people are living normal lives, except for poor Tom, who is living his normal life in prison. When the virus strikes, our heroine, Abby, is one of its victims, but unlike 90% or more of others who are infected, she survives. When she comes out of it, her world is changed forever, but she begins a quest to find her son, Peter, whom she feels may also have survived.

Now, of course, the government is calling for calm, and urging people to wait for them to get control of the situation, but they, of course, are understating the problem. So what else is new! Remember crewmembers on the Titanic telling people there is nothing to worry about? This is basically the same thing. The smart people attempt to get out of Dodge, and slowly Abby's group forms. A reluctant Greg Preston (Paterson Joseph) connects with Abby first, and soon the others connect, too. As they band together and try to get supplies from a supermarket, they are attacked by a group of thugs. They find some supplies, but Tom and Greg accidently expose a young girl, who is with her family in an isolated village, to infection. While the father of the girl resists taking her back in, he eventually comes around. Perhaps the most important development in the series is when Abby meets Samantha Willis (Nikki Amuka-Bird), the last surviving government minister, who is in charge of a small but functional community.

While Abby takes to Samantha initially, she soon realizes Samantha will do anything to preserve order, including employing armed thugs to enforce her will. In the second season, Abby is kidnapped as a few remaining scientists try to make a vaccine from her blood. Along the way, Tom and Greg are enslaved in a coalmine. At the end of the series, Abby gets her son back, but not without help from Tom. Tom confronts a group trying to secure the vaccine in the form of Peter and manages to help free Peter, but Tom appears to sacrifice himself by getting on the group's plane with the idea of taking them out. The series ends here, but it could easily have continued for another season or two. I won't forgive the BBC for ending it here!

While this was hardly a big-budget series, the chemistry between the characters played a large role in its appeal. Moreover, when you look at the scientific aspects of the show, based on some real-world events, this is a very plausible story. As we will see in other films, fears about viruses and contagions will become an increasingly important part of the post-apocalyptic film landscape.

The Walking Dead (American, 2010)

Probably one of the greatest post-apocalyptic TV shows ever is *The Walking Dead*. It premiered in October 2010 on the AMC Network, and has captivated audiences for seven seasons so far. While everybody loves zombie movies, a key to success for this series is a dynamite cast and well-scripted stories. The lead character is former sheriff's deputy Rick Grimes (Andrew Lincoln), but the show is chock full of acting talent. Other key members of the cast include Norman Reedus, Lauren Cohn, Danai Gurira, Steven Yeun, Lennie James, Jon Bernthal, Jeffery DeMunn, Chandler Riggs, Michael Rooker, and Scott Wilson, who scared audiences many years earlier as one of the killers in the film *In Cold Blood*.

The story starts with deputy Rick Grimes getting shot in a shoot-out with some wackos. He ends up in a coma, and wakes up in a zombie apocalypse. Talk about bad dreams! I guess it's implicit that this mess was started by some kind of virus or contagion. However, from my recollection, it is not spelled out that clearly up front. But if you're dealing with flesh-eating zombies, who really cares how it started? After getting some help while he's still injured, he eventually reunites with his family, and some others. They do the modern version of the Trail of Tears.

They always seem to find their way into one bad situation after another. They may get a temporary reprieve, like when they end up on Hershel's (Scott Wilson) farm, but things always end up in the crapper. One of the things that makes this show interesting, but at times hard to deal with, is that key characters come and go. After getting attached to a character, don't be surprised if they get killed off. The losses of Glenn (Steven Yeun) and Hershel were particularly hard to deal with. However, there is always a core group, and new key characters are introduced all the time.

A second key variable in this show's success is that the plot changes, and the group must always face new challenges. At times, fighting zombies is background noise, as the group deals with even more dangerous obstacles. They must face the Governor (David Morrissey), who leads another community but wants Rick and his people gone. There are cannibals to face, and perhaps their biggest challenge is from the Saviors, who are a powerful and sadistic group led by Negan (Jeffrey Dean Morgan) that demand tribute from all the other communities. This show is headed for its eighth season, and shows no sign of slowing down.

Fear the Walking Dead (American, 2015)

The Walking Dead spawned another series, *Fear the Walking Dead* (2015), also produced for AMC, which is into its third season at this writing. While it's a spin-off from the original *Walking Dead* show, *Fear the Walking Dead* takes place mostly in California and Mexico. OK, so where would you want to survive the zombie apocalypse: the South or Mexico and California? Could you imagine dealing with zombie governor Jerry Brown on top of the apocalypse? Yikes, I'd rather be with Rick and his gang!

To be clear, *Fear* is a zombie apocalypse series, but as is often the case, I'm not always sure what started this apocalypse. Now, it's usually some stupid thing the government does, but you never know. The plot is basically following a group of survivors that includes a semi-dysfunctional family. The interaction between the characters is good, and watching them survive all kinds of crap is entertaining. I mean, these guys manage to break in and out of a prison, survive a zombie air crash site, and all sorts of wacko groups and crazies. They also prove they can be as ruthless as is necessary to survive. They are willing to leave people behind to save their own asses, including leaving someone on a life raft in the middle of the ocean, turning zombies loose on people to get away, and destroying safe compounds to avoid being stopped or caught.

Key cast members include Madison Clark (Kim Dickens), who is a very nice mom, but is tough as nails; her daughter, Alicia (Alycia Debman-Carey); Madison's son, Nick (Frank Dilane); and her husband, Travis Manawa (Tim Curtis), a very nice guy in a very nasty situation. Like *The Walking Dead*, when family members are lost they never give up on finding them. And, also like *The Walking Dead*, they have no problem getting rid of key characters to keep it interesting. At the start of the third season they got rid of Travis! It's a good show, but not quite at the level of *The Walking Dead*.

Z Nation (American, 2014)

A bit further down the food chain is *Z Nation*. A couple of years after a virus initiates—so what else is new—a zombie apocalypse, which has killed off most of the population, a group of survivors must transport a character named Murphy (Keith Allan) from New York to a CDC facility in California. Murphy, having received some kind of vaccine, is now immune to the zombie virus. Bottom line, Murphy represents the cure, but he is kind of a jerk, and always seems to make life difficult for his handlers. This is kind of zombie-lite, with a campy style that at times can be entertaining. However, even though it has four seasons under its belt, I never regarded this as a must-see show.

Zombie Hunters: City of the Dead (American, 2007)

NR

While not a well-known production, *Zombie Hunters: City of The Dead* deserves credit as the first zombie TV series. Featured on public access stations, some sample episodes may also be available on the Internet. At the time of this writing, there are ten completed episodes out there, with two more to go. This is an "indie" film production that may not be big budget, but can be entertaining. This series preceded *The Walking Dead*, and what it may lack in funding, it more than makes up for in creativity. Patrick Devaney is the director and producer of the series, and also a character. He and Christopher Murphy, Rick Martinez, and Teri Hansen play key characters. The story takes place in New York City, and our heroes battle zombies and extremist groups throughout the city. The series gets better with each episode, and the make-up work by Michael Scardillo is very impressive. Since I had a minor role in the production of one of the episodes, I thought it would be unfair to go overboard with comments on this series.

After Armageddon (American, 2010)

Finally, I wanted to comment on the serious side of post-apocalyptic entertainment. By now, everybody probably knows about the *Doomsday Preppers* show. Well, I'm not going to talk about that, but I did want to comment on a History Channel release in 2010 called *After Armageddon*. This is a docudrama that chronicles the life of the Johnson family after some worldwide pandemic. What makes this so interesting is that you have all kinds of experts weighing in on the real consequences of such an event, and the poor Johnson family is stuck acting it out. So what really happens when there is no power, food, medicine, or water? And how is the human race going to react to this? Not surprisingly, not well.

What makes this show so interesting is that it shows not only the destruction of our society and way of life, but also how people may cope to survive. Basically, we end up in the 19th century, using those farming and medical techniques, and bartering to get by. Our hero, Chris Johnson (Rob Hartz), who gets his family through the initial crisis and establishes them in a solid farming community, ends up dying from a simple cut, because there are no antibiotics available. The experts say we would be back in the 1800s. So expect those death rates to be consistent with that kind of medical care. If you want to get a fix on the realities of the apocalypse, you should watch this production.

Supervolcano (British, 2005)

The Brits have been scaring the crap out of me for almost 40 years, and the BBC production of *Supervolcano*, released on TV in 2005, is no exception. The Brits started their scare campaign with me with *The Day of the Triffids,* and really ratcheted up with *Threads* and *Survivor,* but *Supervolcano* really made me run for cover. You know those docudramas seem so real, and this was no exception. Hell, they started the film by saying this was a true story, "it just hasn't happened yet."

The story starts out with some different points of view about the Yellowstone Supervolcano, which some feel is on the verge of eruption. Scientist Rick Lieberman (Michael Riley), who works at Yellowstone, tries to get people to keep things in perspective. While some are running off telling folks what could happen if Yellowstone blows, Rick warns people they are getting ahead of themselves. Although a short time later, he has his wife and child on a plane to London. But when Wendy Reiss (Rebecca Jenkins), the head of FEMA, visits with Rick for the first time, he tries to give her an honest picture, including the worst-case scenario. However, he reminds her that nobody really knows when it will happen, or how bad it will be.

Well, when it happens, it's very bad. A series of earthquakes set off an eruption that spews out smoke and ash over most of the United States. Some people try to get out early to Canada and Mexico, but, of course, Mexico closes its borders. Roads are clogged and most of our interstates become parking lots, and air travel is severely limited. Rick, who is on an airplane, barely manages to escape a crash because of the ash, and ends up walking to a small military base to try to help.

Thousands are dead, an estimated 25 million are trapped in the danger zone, and things don't look too good for anyone else, either. FEMA has told people to stay in place, and help will come. Rick tells the FEMA team that they must get people to "walk to life" or they will starve and die in place. FEMA agrees, and while there is a massive loss of life, people are saved because of Rick's advice. Rick makes it out, and manages to ride over Yellowstone to see the devastation. The net effect is that 80% of the U.S. is covered in ash, with 20% totally uninhabitable. I can't even imagine the economic impact. This was a frightening picture of what nature can do, and the film gets your attention far more than the usual zombie apocalypse could ever do. Not for the faint of heart!

Containment (American, 2016)

A rather respectable TV series that presents a scary virus scenario is
Containment, which first aired in April 2016, but I have just seen it recently on Netflix. This series shares some similarities with a British film,
also called *Containment*, which was released a year earlier. The American version presents a much broader challenge with respect to dealing
with a dangerous virus. While the focus of this program is on develop-
ments in Atlanta, it represents a microcosm of the potential effects on a
global basis. Yes, it's just one city, but as the title implies, this could be
a catastrophic event for mankind. Any time you're dealing with a virus
that has a 100% mortality rate, you've got a big problem. I hate to say
it, but these virus movies scare the hell out of me, probably because the
risks seem so real, and they underscore how fragile life is.

This virus appears to be brought into the country by a Syrian man,
who almost immediately infects a doctor at the hospital, along with
his own family. The doctor and her boyfriend die in short order, and a
search is started immediately to find Patient Zero. As we see later on, it
wasn't the Syrian guy but some wacko American playing around with
viruses. In any case, this is serious stuff, and the government sends in
Dr. Sabine Lommers (Claudia Black), a no-nonsense kind of gal who
has experience in managing serious viral outbreaks around the world.
She gets to work with police major Alex "Lex" Carnahan (David Gyasi),
a rising star in the Atlanta police department, who is both decent and
smart. For the record, the series puts heavy emphasis on the relationships of key characters. One of these is Carnahan's relationship with his
girlfriend, Jana (Christina Marie Moses).

Upon arrival, Lommers decides a quarantine of part of the city is
the only way to stop the virus. They have no cure, and containment is
the best option. She enlists Carnahan's help, but not surprisingly, things
head south real fast. What do you expect, this is a show about a virus
with a 100% mortality rate!

The little stories include problems in Carnahan's relationship with
Jana, his friend Jake's budding romance with Katie Frank (Kristen
Gutoskia), and a young pregnant woman trying to reunite with her boy-

friend. But despite the "you have nothing to worry about, so just stay calm" message from the authorities, people start to panic, and social order in the quarantined area breaks down.

So, how bad is it? Well, a bunch of kids are stuck in a hospital because they get exposed on a field trip, bands of thugs steal food to sell to others, people in the quarantined area are dropping like flies, and the hospital is running out of lab rats. Carnahan gets fed up with his PR role of telling people they have nothing to worry about, as they bring in trailer containers to seal the area off.

As the show winds down, Lommers blames Dr. Cannerts (George Young), who has been working tirelessly to find a cure. In reality, it appears that Lommers knew all along how the virus spread, which is why she was so prepared to deal with it. Once again, it seems like this outbreak was caused by people messing with stuff they should not have been. Carnahan decides to reunite with Jana in the quarantine zone. Katie dies of the virus, ending Jake's hope of a relationship with her. The show ends with people still stuck in the quarantine part of the city, but what happens next we may never know, as the show was cancelled after season one. It is an engaging story, and parts seemed almost too realistic. I'm not sure how much longer they could have kept it going, but I think a second season would have worked.

Conclusion

A s I said at the outset, post-apocalyptic films have been around for over 100 years, and I suspect they will continue to find an important place among sci-fi movies. However, I do think that zombie and similar films have gotten a little stale, and there is a need for new themes in the post-apocalyptic film genre. Perhaps more attention will be given to EMPs or climate change. Terrorism could also represent a possible storyline for some of these films.

While the above comments suggest that some apocalyptic storylines are getting a little old, there is always room for improvement and rejuvenation. But let's be clear; special effects and big-name actors are often not enough to make a good movie; only good stories can do that. Films like *These Final Hours*, *When Worlds Collide*, *Mad Max*, and *Panic in Year Zero* prove the importance of good storytelling. Nevertheless, after going through over 100 of these films, the success of this theme has brought about the "rip off" effect as some filmmakers try to capitalize on the theme, but bring very little value. As with anything else, imitation may be the highest form of flattery, but cheap and poorly executed imitations flatter no one, and only disappoint.

While this is nothing new, perhaps more attention could be paid to how survivors rebuild the world. For many viewers, watching how people cope with a new and hostile world is the most interesting part of the movie. Perhaps we fantasize about what we would do under similar circumstances. How many of us would be as resourceful as Harry Baldwin (*Panic in Year Zero*), or Max (*Road Warrior*), or even the man (*The Road*)? These are questions we hope we never have to answer. But I believe that's the attraction of these films. Intellectually, we want to know how we would survive the impossible.

Be careful of what you wish for, as you may not like the answer. Interestingly, this issue reminds me of a conversation I had with an old anthropology professor many years ago. He reminded me that the more complex the society, the simpler the individual; whereas, the simpler the society, the more complex the person. What he was really saying was that people in more simple societies have greater survival skills. He told me that a South American Indian could easily survive in our world, but we could not survive in his. How many of us can hunt, gather, make shelters, understand what plants to use for medical purposes, or even fashion tools for any of these endeavors? I think we all know the answer to that question. In our films, we see that only a few of the very resourceful can survive a post-apocalyptic scenario, and if we are honest, we know that probably doesn't include most of us.

One of the more significant aspects of post-apocalyptic movies is that we are often the ones to blame for the "end of the world." Nuclear war, climate change, economic collapse, EMPs, bio-weapons, and man-made viruses are reflections of our own folly. Of the 100 plus films discussed in this book, close to 60% indicate the source of the apocalypse was human. Imagine what that does for our self-image! Still, it's hard to argue with the facts, and, I guess, if the shoe fits... So far, I haven't seen anything that would challenge this conclusion, nor evidence that we have really learned anything from the message.

In any event, for whatever reason, these films have captured our collective imagination. They fill us with wonder and fear, and at a very deep level, they make the world an even scarier place. As I have said along the way, these films even mirror events in the real world. It's not lost on us that a meteor took out the dinosaurs, or that we can be devastated by disease and sickness.

Basically, these films remind us we are feeble creatures and never really in control. This is compounded by the fact that we are often on our own. Governments, electric grids, and food and medical supplies fail us. Simply put, we are often alone to deal with the destructive nature of human folly or the forces of nature. We are at the mercy of comets, viruses, blackouts, wars, and even zombies. No matter how strong or resourceful we may think we are, the apocalypse is the great equalizer. It's hard to hide from radiation, sickness, or natural disasters. In the end, the End wins. As much as many of us watch and enjoy these movies, somewhere in the back of our minds we keep saying to ourselves, "It's only a movie!"

Appendix A: Top-Ten Rankings

Top Ten Post-Apocalyptic Films

1. The Time Machine (1960).
2. Planet of the Apes (1968)
3. Night of the Living Dead (1968)
4. Things to Come (1936)
5. The Day After Tomorrow (2004)
6. When Worlds Collide (1951)
7. Soylent Green (1973)
8. Threads (1984)
9. On the Beach (1959)
10. I Am Legend (2007)

Ten Worst Post-Apocalyptic Films

1. The Last Woman on Earth (1960)
2. Robot Monster (1953)
3. Day the World Ended (1955)
4. The Lost Missile (1958)
5. The Aftermath (1982)
6. Warlords of the 21st Century (1982)
7. To Survive (2014)
8. Where Have all the People Gone? (1974)
9. Collapse (2011)
10. 20 Years Later (2008)

Appendix B: Post-Apocalyptic Film Subject Index

Trying to categorize these films is a bit challenging, to say the least. It turned out to be a very subjective, and at times limiting, process. Many of the zombie flicks could have just as easily fallen into the virus category, and vice versa. Bottom line: I did the best I could, and I apologize for somewhat broad categories. On the Chapter list, I used a little more flexibility with the classifications.

Aliens
The Day the Earth Stood Still
Independence Day
The Invasion
Invasion of the Body Snatchers
The Lost Missile
Robot Monster
10 Cloverfield Lane
War of the Worlds

Bio-Weapon
The Crazies
Parts Per Billion

Diseases/Viruses*
After Armageddon
The Andromeda Strain**
Carriers
Contagion
Containment
I Am Legend
Last Man on Earth
Omega Man
Plague
Refuge
The Stand
Survivors
Virus

Economic/Social Collapse
Escape from New York
Mad Max
The Road Warrior
The Survivalist

Mutant Monsters/Monsters
Cloverfield
Them!

Natural Disaster/Cosmic Calamity/ Ecological Collapse

Arctic Blast
Armageddon
Asteroid vs Earth
Crack in the World
The Colony
The Core
The Day After Tomorrow
The Day of the Triffids
Deep Impact
Deluge
The End of the World (1916)
End of the World (1931)
The Final Wave
The Happening
Judge Dredd
The Last Wave
Last Woman on Earth
Logan's Run
Millennium
Night of the Comet
The Road
Soylent Green
Supervolcano
These Final Hours
2012
Twilight Zone (Season 3: The Midnight Sun)
Tycus
Waterworld
Where Have All the People Gone
Without Warning
When Worlds Collide

Nuclear War/War

Aftermath
Alas, Babylon
Atomic Attack
The Book of Eli
A Boy and His Dog
The Day After
Day the World Ended
Dr. Strangelove or: How I Learned to Stop Worrying and Love the Bomb
Fail-Safe
Five
Hunger Games
Jericho
Land of Doom
On the Beach
The World, the Flesh and the Devil
The Time Machine
This Is Not a Test
Panic in Year Zero
Planet of the Apes
The Terminator
Terminator 2
Testament
Things to Come
Threads
20 Years After
Twilight Zone (Season 1: Time Enough at Last)
Twilight Zone (Season 3: Two)
Twilight Zone (Season 5: The Old Man in the Cave)
Warlords of the 21st Century (Battletruck)
World Without End

Technology/EMP

Cell
Goodbye World
Into the Forest

Unknown
The Day
To Survive

Zombie
Autumn
Collapse
Dawn of the Dead (1978)
Dawn of the Dead (2004)
Diary of the Dead
Extinction
Fear the Walking Dead
Here Alone
Land of the Dead
Night of the Living Dead
Pandemic
Resident Evil
Resident Evil: Apocalypse
Resident Evil: Extinction
The Walking Dead
28 Days Later
28 Weeks Later
World War Z
Z Nation
Zombie Apocalypse
Zombie Hunters: City of the Dead
Zombieland

* Zombie viruses excluded
** Alien virus

Appendix C: Complete Film List and Rankings

n an attempt to provide some useful feedback to potential film viewers, I have rated each of the films I covered in this book. The ratings go from one to five exploding worlds (as shown below), with five being the best. Almost a third of the films are average to below average; the other two thirds run from watchable to really worth seeing. Of course this is subjective, and one man's apocalypse may be another's stroll in the park.

Chapt. Page #	Film	Release Date	Category	Rating
1 4	The End of the World	1916	Comet	(5 icons)
1 5	End of World	1931	Comet	NR
1 6	Deluge	1933	Earth-quakes	(4 icons)
1 7	Things to Come	1936	War	(5 icons)
2 9	Five	1951	Nuclear War	(5 icons)
2 10	When Worlds Collide	1951	Meteor	(5 icons)
2 11	War of the Worlds	1953	Aliens	(5 icons)
2 12	Robot Monster	1953	Aliens	(2 icons)
2 13	Them*	1954	Nuclear Fallout	(4 icons)
2 13	Invasion of the Body Snatchers*	1956	Aliens	(5 icons)
2 14	The Day the Earth Stood Still*	1951	Aliens	(4 icons)
2 14	World Without End	1956	Nuclear War	(4 icons)
2 15	Day the World Ended	1955	Nuclear War	(2 icons)

Chapt. Page #	Film	Release Date	Category	Rating
2 16	The World, The Flesh and the Devil	1959	Nuclear War	
2 17	The Lost Missile	1958	Aliens	
2 18	On The Beach	1959	Nuclear War	
3 19	The Time Machine	1960	War	
3 21	The Last Woman on Earth	1960	Ecological	
3 21	Last Man on Earth	1964	Virus	
3 22	Panic in Year Zero	1962	Nuclear War	
3 23	This is Not a Test	1962	Nuclear War	
3 24	Day of the Triffids	1963	Cosmic	
3 25	Dr. Strangelove	1964	Nuclear War	
3 25	Fail-Safe	1964	Nuclear War	
3 26	Crack in the World	1965	Human Folly	
3 27	Planet of the Apes	1968	Nuclear War	

Chapt. Page #	Film	Release Date	Category	Rating
3 29	Night of theLiving Dead	1968	Zombie	
4 32	The Andromeda Strain	1971	Virus**	
4 33	The Crazies	1972	Bio Weapon	
4 35	The Omega Man	1971	Virus	
4 36	Soylent Green	1973	Climate Change	
4 37	The Last Wave	1977	Tidal Wave	
4 38	Dawn of the Dead	1978	Zombie	
4 39	A Boy and His Dog	1975	Nuclear War	
4 40	Logan's Run	1976	Overpopu-lation	
4 41	Mad Max	1979	Collapse	
5 43	Night of the Comet	1984	Cosmic	
5 44	Land of Doom	1986	Nuclear War	
5 45	Virus	1980	Virus	

Chapt. Page #	Film	Release Date	Category	Rating
5 46	The Road Warrior	1981	Collapse	
5 46	Warlords of the 21st Century	1982	Nuclear War	
5 47	The Aftermath	1982	Nuclear War	
5 48	The Terminator	1984	Nuclear War	
5 49	Escape from New York	1981	Collapse	
5 51	Millennium	1989	Polution	
6 53	Deep Impact	1998	Meteor	
6 55	Armageddon	1998	Meteor	
6 56	Terminator 2	1991	War	
6 57	Waterworld	1995	Climate Change	
6 58	Independence Day	1996	Aliens	
6 59	Judge Dredd	1995	Polution	
6 61	Tycus	1998	Comet	

Chapt. Page #	Film	Release Date	Category	Rating
7 63	The Day After Tomorrow	2004	Climate Change	
7 64	The Colony	2013	Climate Change	
7 65	Arctic Blast	2010	Climate Change	
7 66	The Core	2013	Earth Problem	
7 67	2012	2009	Cosmic	
7 68	The Book of Eli	2010	Nuclear War	
7 69	Cloverfield	2008	Monster	
7 71	The Invasion	2007	Aliens	
7 72	The Happening	2008	Plants	
7 74	20 Years After	2008	Nuclear War	
7 75	I Am Legend	2007	Virus	
7 77	Contagion	2011	Virus	
7 78	Carriers	2009	Virus	

Chapt. Page #	Film	Release Date	Category	Rating
7 80	Plague	2015	Virus	
7 81	Refuge	2013	Virus	
7 82	Parts Per Billion	2014	Bio Weapon	
7 83	Into The Forest	2015	Blackout	
7 85	Hunger Games	2012	War	
7 86	The Road	2009	Ecological Collapse	
7 87	The Day	2011	Unkown	
7 89	To Survive	2014	Unkown	
7 89	These Final Hours	2013	Cosmic	
7 90	Cell	2016	Technology	
7 92	Goodbye World	2013	Technology	
7 93	10 Colverfield Lane	2016	Aliens	
7 94	The Survivalist	2015	Economic Collapse	

Chapt. Page #	Film	Release Date	Category	Rating
8 96	28 Days Later	2002	Zombie	
8 98	28 Weeks Later	2007	Zombie	
8 98	Dawn of the Dead	2004	Zombie	
8 100	Land of the Dead	2005	Zombie	
8 101	Diary of the Dead	2007	Zombie	
8 103	Resident Evil	2002	Zombie	
8 103	Resident Evil: Apocalypse	2004	Zombie	
8 104	Resident Evil: Extinction	2007	Zombie	
8 105	Zombie Apoica-lypse	2011	Zombie	
8 106	Autumn	2009	Zombie	
8 107	World War Z	2013	Zombie	
8 109	Extinction	2015	Zombie	
8 110	Collapse	2011	Zombie	

Chapt. Page #	Film	Release Date	Category	Rating
8 111	Pandemic	2016	Zombie	
8 112	Here Alone	2016	Zombie	
8 113	Zombieland	2009	Zombie	
9 115	Playhouse 90: Alas Babylon	1960	Nuclear War	
9 117	The Motorola Television Hour; Atomic Attack	1954	Nuclear War	
9 118	Twlight Zone: Time Enough at Last	1959	Nuclear War	
9 118	Twlight Zone: The Midnight Sun	1961	Cosmic	
9 119	Twlight Zone: Two	1961	War	
9 120	Twlight Zone: The Old Man in the Cave	1963	Nuclear War	
9 121	Where Have All the People gone	1974	Solar Flares	
9 122	Threads	1984	Nuclear War	
9 123	Teastament	1983	Nuclear War	

Chapt. Page #	Film	Release Date	Category	Rating
9 124	The Day after	1983	Nuclear War	
9 125	Jericho	2006	Nuclear War	
9 126	Without Warning	1994	Meteor	
9 126	Asteroid vs. Earth	2014	Meteor	
9 127	The Stand	1994	Virus	
9 128	Surviors	2008	Virus	
9 130	The Walking Dead	2010	Zombie	
9 131	Fear of the Walking Dead	2015	Zombie	
9 132	Z Nation	2014	Zombie	
9 132	Zombie Hunters: City of the Dead	2007	Zombie	NR***
9 133	After Armageddon	2010	Pandemic	
9 133	Supervolcano	2005	Eruption	

Chapt. Page #	Film	Release Date	Category	Rating
9 135	Containment	2016	Virus	🕷🕷🕷🕷

* Apocalypse Lite

** Alien Virus

*** I had a small role in the production of one episode so did not feel it right to provide a rating

About the Author

Originally trained as a sociologist, Nick decided to pursue a career in Corporate Finance. He worked on Wall Street for almost 35 years, and was a Managing Director at a major credit rating firm. Part of his role included being a company spokesman for key issues, and he frequently interacted with the media on emerging trends in finance. Several of his published articles received coverage in *The New York Times*, *The Wall Street Journal*, *USA Today*, and *Financial Times*. Nick was often a guest speaker at many Corporate Finance and High Yield Investment conferences. A series of articles he orchestrated and coauthored, *The Leveraging of America*, won his team the McGraw-Hill Corporate Achievement award in 2008. That series has been included in the curriculum at some business schools. Since his retirement from corporate finance, he has entered the rare book business, and is currently a member of the Antiquarian Booksellers' Association of America. He specializes in books relating to American and African-American history. With his wife, Mary, and sons David and Paul, Nick resides in New Jersey. Nick's family shares his love of science fiction films, and they frequently attend sci-fi conventions in the region.